Retirement

Planning

What You Don't Know Will Hurt You!

Written By

Kris Keush

Retirement Planning

Retirement Planning

Copyright © 2023

All Rights Reserved

Retirement Planning

CONTENTS

Chapter 1

Introduction

Retirement is when an individual leaves the workforce behind permanently. Every country and state has varying laws regarding retirement. The typical age to retire in the United States is 65. Nations also have different kinds of national pensions or other benefit systems to complement the retiree's incomes.

Retirement is one the most significant financial goals for people – especially those working the 9-5 grind. Unfortunately, there exists a great layer of ambiguity over the whole thing, giving rise to questions and confusion in the minds of people.

As a result, when the time comes for them to retire, they are unprepared and clueless. Not only that, but they jump into their retirement period without planning it out. When that happens, they lack the finances and resources needed to cover their expenditures.

In scenarios like these, retirement can become more of a challenge that contradicts its whole point. And just like that, the safety net that most people ever look forward to since joining the corporate world or going down the entrepreneurial road.

This is one of the reasons people should invest in educating themselves more about retirement; what to expect when you're retiring, what happens when they retire, and what their options are.

Things get difficult when you stop getting your regular monthly income. Therefore, it is incumbent to do your retirement planning so that when the time comes, you're fully covered and have financial freedom. **Planning for all aspects from an early age is the right thing to do.** In addition to that, along with planning, you must make sure to gain as much information and knowledge about your retirement policies and pension plans so that when you retire, you know exactly what you have and don't make the mistakes that end up putting you in a messy situation.

Being prepared can take you a long way and help you maximize your retirement earnings.

The world that we live in is fast-paced and ever-changing. At first glance, there isn't much that has changed when it comes to retirement planning. It's straightforward; first, we work. Then, we save. And then, when the time is right, we retire.

But things are definitely not the way they appear to be on the surface. The world has changed significantly over time. With an economic crisis at hand, while the world is still reeling from a health crisis in the form of the **COVID-19** pandemic, the future looks bleak. On top of that, inflation is at an all-time high. With all these factors weighing in, it is safe to say that living costs have surged and skyrocketed.

This is a cause of concern for all: those who gain the benefits from retirement and those who are funding it. Perhaps, this is why we have seen a shift from traditional company pensions towards defined-contribution retirement plans in the US. Moving the burden of funding retirements from employers toward employees themselves is a smart move for companies. Again, this creates a lack of clarity when it comes to retirement.

It is no surprise that retirees often face financial concerns (along with other non-financial issues such as deteriorating health and boredom). To combat these concerns, it is vital to be prepared for the shift from an employee to a retiree. To do so, one must make hard decisions and tough calls when needed.

The purpose of writing this book is to educate you about making a smooth transition into retirement when the time comes, and for that, you must set things straight from the start. Many people make the grave mistake of thinking about retirement-related issues a year or two before they retire. As per the Employee Benefits Security Administration Department, only half of Americans have calculated how much they need to save for retirement. Now consider that in 2020, more than a quarter of private industry workers with access to a defined contribution plan (such as a 401(k) plan) did not anticipate (please note that there are several different retirements plans and options. We shall be covering those later in the book as well). This is a huge mistake as an average person spends 20 years in retirement; therefore, enough funds should be allocated, and saving from an early age helps a lot!

You should know how much retirement income to expect per month. This will help you figure out how much you need to save. You need to be very disciplined about it and only withdraw as much as budgeted for the month. You do not withdraw any of your retirement savings (emergency savings).

Although plenty of books are readily available in the market on the subject of retirement planning, this book takes it a step further. This book is not only easy to read and understand, but it will also educate readers about all possible retirement plans and options. This way, people who plan on retiring in the future can arm themselves with all the facts before making an informed decision about the path that they want to choose.

This book is a one-stop-for-all. It doesn't matter if you don't know the first thing about retirement plans or if you know everything about it. It doesn't matter if you've saved funds for when the time comes for you to retire; or if you have made investments for your future. It doesn't matter if your savings are meager or non-existent.

This book provides incoming-planning options and action plans with easy, to-do steps for all, regardless of where you are starting from.

Not only will this book enlighten you about every retirement plan there is, but it will also help you convert your money into sustainable income. This way, you don't have to worry about your retirement plan because you shall have a safety net to fall back on. You will have a long-term care program with large funds that won't be affected by possible large expenses or emergency spending that you may incur.

Before we dive further into the book, let's take a look at a few steps you must take.

1. Start Saving, Keep Saving, And Stick to Your Goals

If you are already saving for retirement or another goal, keep going! You know that saving is a rewarding habit. If you're not saving, it's time to get started. Start small if you have to, and try to gradually increase the amount you save each month. The sooner you start saving, the more time your money must grow. Make saving for retirement a priority. Devise a plan, stick to it, and set goals. Remember, it's never too early or too late to start saving.

2. Know Your Retirement Needs

Retirement is expensive. Experts estimate that you will need 70 to 90 percent of your preretirement income to maintain your standard of living when you stop working. Take charge of your financial future. The key to a secure retirement is to plan ahead.

3. Contribute To Your Employer's Retirement Savings Plan

If your employer offers a retirement savings plan, sign up and contribute all you can. This will reduce your taxes will be lower allow your company to kick in more, and the automatic deductions will make it easier. Over time, compound interest and tax deferrals significantly affect the amount you will accumulate. Find out about your plan. For example, how much would you need to contribute to get the full employer contribution, and how long would you need to stay in the plan to get that money? Also, investigate other options for a retirement income stream such as an IUL, Life Insurance, Annuity, etc. don't stop your 401K, but adding other streams of retirement planning will help you when you retire. Plus, it is great to know you have a guarantee set amount when you retire.

4. Learn About Your Employer's Retirement Plan.

If your employer has a traditional pension/retirement plan, check to see if you are covered by the plan and understand how it works. Ask for an individual benefit statement to see what your benefit is worth. Before changing jobs, find out what will happen to your pension/retirement benefit. Learn what benefits you may have from a previous employer. Find out if you will be entitled to benefits from your spouse's plan.

5. Consider Basic Investment Principles

How you save can be as important as how much you save. Inflation and the type of investments you make are important in how much you'll have saved at retirement. Know how your savings or pension/retirement plan is invested. Learn about your plan's investment options and ask questions. Put your savings in different types of investments. i.e., 401K, IRA, Roth, IUL, Life Insurance, Annuities, etc. By diversifying this way, you are more likely to reduce risk and improve return. Your investment mix may change over time depending on several factors, such as your age, goals, and financial circumstances. Financial security and knowledge go hand in hand.

6. Don't Touch Your Retirement Savings

If you withdraw your retirement savings now, you'll lose principal and interest. You may lose tax benefits or must pay withdrawal penalties. If you change jobs, leave your savings invested in your current retirement plan, or roll them over to another investment or your new employer's plan.

7. Put Money into An Individual Retirement Account

As 401k and **IRA** have a place in your retirement portfolio, you need to make sure you have a major part of your retirement portfolio placed in an investment that you will not lose your money in and you can't outlive. Starting out, put money into an IUL or other insurance products as you are working. The sooner you start this, the better. This acts as another retirement income that is tax-deferred when taking your money and has a set amount that you can't outlive, like a pension plan. As you transition to getting closer to retirement, you need to start looking at switching some of your assets from your **401K** into an **FIA** (*Fixed Index Annuity*) and other forms of secure forms of retirement investments. This will prevent you from losing your money in a down market and have a better idea of a plan for retirement. If you have not already got a Life Insurance policy with Living Benefits, now is the time to start looking into this. This is a life insurance policy that pays you while you are still alive with money left over to pass on to loved ones.

8. Find Out About Your Social Security Benefits

On average, Social Security retirement benefits replace 40 percent of preretirement income for retirement beneficiaries. You may be able to estimate your benefit by using the retirement estimator on the Social Security Administration's website.

Retirement is both – a big change and a challenge. It is a new phase of life; you need to plan for it as early as possible. While no one knows how long they will live or even make it to retirement age, it is wise to do the first step (which most Americans make the grave mistake of skipping): start by planning.

Therefore, I call all employed people, especially young people, to consider focusing on their skill development right after they get into employment so it gets easy for them to go independent as they grow older. The next few chapters will be hard to read – in terms of the advice they give and the decisions they ask you to make – but do it for your sake!

Chapter 2

Retirement Plans

Many pre-retirees and retirees wonder if they are on the right financial route to a prosperous retirement. The structure for determining the answer is provided in this chapter. We want to establish whether adequate assets exist to satisfy the anticipated retirement liabilities, including desirable reserves for spending shocks. We calculate the size of the household assets and liabilities.

A concerted effort is required to develop a realistic retirement budget that accounts for our ongoing requirements and preferences. In order to prevent retirement expenditures from becoming unmanageable, an effort must be made to develop a realistic retirement budget. The retiree must be completely certain that the plan can also manage spending shocks and other retirement risks.

I also think about what I might do if my retirement is not well-funded and my assets fall short of my liabilities.

We must evaluate how to effectively combine retirement income tools and methods to optimize the balance between these objectives in ways consistent with our own retirement income style.

Developing a retirement income plan includes defining retirement goals and effectively fulfilling and preserving those goals against retirement hazards.

Do you have enough assets to fund tools to help you meet your goals and manage your risks in retirement?

The fundamental financial goal in retirement is to fund your ongoing budgeted expenses for the rest of your life and have a retirement plan that you can't outlive. The budget or spending plan relates to longevity and lifestyle goals, though we will not make this distinction immediately. Budgeting is not always enjoyable, but there are tools available to help simplify the process.

It is common to be nervous about whether you have saved enough for retirement when you do not know what you have been spending and what amount of spending will help you support a comfortable lifestyle.

By determining a budget, it becomes easier to assess retirement preparedness. Perhaps you already have sufficient savings, which could be a great comfort. If underfunded, you can design a plan for how to respond. Decisions include delaying retirement, reducing budgeted expenses, or assuming a higher rate of return on your assets. There will be more clarity.

A significant source of uncertainty can now be better understood and managed.

Budgeting for retirement is challenging because many costs may shift as you enter retirement. New retirees go through a substantial lifestyle change. Adjustments may be required to consider changes occurring at retirement, even for people who have kept meticulous records of their yearly spending over the years before retiring. This is particularly true for retirees who move as a part of their retirement.

Budgeting for retirement is keeping track of your spending and planning how those costs are expected to alter. You will require a plausible estimation of the starting costs. How much do you plan to spend annually after you reach retirement? Will your overall retirement expenditures increase slower or faster than inflation?

Your spending habits may vary in retirement, but you must remember where you started and unearth any expenditure you would not have considered otherwise. Although inflation has been modest in recent years, you may want to alter your previous spending to account for growing prices and make those expenses more indicative of today's purchasing power. Once you have a sense of your recent expenditures, it will be easy to adapt these figures for what may happen in retirement.

A short list of expenditure categories to include in your budget might be considered. This collection of general expenditure categories and subcategories may be used to estimate your expenses.

Some retirees may escape the issue of shifting expenditure by thinking that their budget would simply expand in line with consumer price inflation throughout their retirement. This is a generally cautious assumption that might also give a mechanism to budget assets for unexpected expenditure shocks, as retirement spending is expected to fall with age. Early in their retirement, retirees are more active and have more discretionary income for areas such as travel and dining.

Although retirement spending tends to maintain pace with inflation, retirees will ultimately slow down and become less active. Spending no longer keeps pace with inflation and may even fall nominally.

Do you also have measurable legacy objectives in addition to your budget?

Is leaving a specific legacy essential to you, or do you accept that your legacy will be whatever is ultimately left behind without having to make any precise plans?

Legacy objectives might be set for relatives, charities, or other organizations. The legacy can also be divided into one-time gifts included in the budget or a fixed sum given upon death. Additionally, life insurance may be a helpful instrument for leaving a certain bequest sum upon death. Suppose one has particular legacy objectives in mind. In that case, it is crucial to consider these goals when going through the budgeting process.

Another budgeting challenge is distinguishing between lifestyle and longevity expenditures. The primary retirement expenditures are set and unchangeable. However, this may not be the total budget. Some costs may be deemed discretionary. Is there a basic spending level you could handle comfortably while still feeling that your retirement is going well, even if it does not contain everything?

With a budget in place, we next need to consider the overall retirement cost. A problem with determining the cost of funding financial goals in retirement is that retirees must manage differing risks. Retirement risks include longevity risk, market risk, and spending shocks. Even if the planned budget is exactly right and the precise amount of future annual spending is known, retirees do not know how long they will live and what future market returns will be.

The retirement budget will cost more as one lives longer or experiences poor market returns. Spending shocks add further uncertainty around how much will need to be spent. When spending shocks are realized, the cost of retirement grows further. At some point, retirement costs may exceed the available assets. The funded ratio provides a relatively simple way to understand if one is prepared to fund their lifetime retirement goals based on their decisions related to these risks.

The funded ratio is based on the retirement balance sheet's value of assets and liabilities. It does not report a probability of success for the financial plan like many financial planning software programs. It is much simpler as it uses a fixed rate of return assumption as a "discount rate" that converts the value of future cash flows into today's dollars. When the discount rate is chosen conservatively, the funded ratio lets us see whether the goals of a retirement plan can be met without taking market risk.

A funded ratio of 1, implying a funded status of 100%, means that retirees have just enough assets to meet their liabilities. Overfunded and underfunded retirees have more or less than this.

The next stage is to determine the current values for these cash flows for the balance sheet once the cash flows are established and a planning age has been chosen. These computations are shown in the row with present values.

In order to account for the fact that fewer assets are required today to cover future costs, these present values must be calculated using a discount rate to lower the value of future cash flows (*assuming a positive discount rate*).

Suppose I anticipate that my assets will increase in value over time. In that case, I may reduce the money I need to set away today to fund future expenses. The amount of assets that would need to be set aside today to fund the future cash flows is the present value.

The funded ratio is then calculated by adding these cash flow present values to the current values of other assets and liabilities to create the entire retirement balance sheet.

On the asset side, one can choose to put off retirement and continue working. Delaying retirement is the most effective way to increase retirement sustainability if it is feasible to continue working. It allows for more growth and savings, a shorter subsequent retirement to fund, and a strengthened ability to delay Social Security, possibly even increasing the primary insurance amount. This plan is affected by increased work by including the present value of future profits as an additional asset.

If the plan is underfunded, take initial steps to determine a course of action to improve the comfort that one has a reasonably funded plan.

Chapter 3

Portfolio Diversification and Its Importance in Planning for Retirement.

An essential aspect of a retirement plan that includes portfolio distributions as a spending source is the basics of sustainable portfolio distributions in the face of longevity and market risk. This will be our focal point for this chapter.

William Bergen's research is a foundation for studying retirement spending using safe withdrawal rates based on historical data. He introduced the concept of **SAFEMAX**. Basing it around the worst case that the US has suffered through. This was later translated in terms of portfolio success rates for different strategies, with the idea becoming to focus on withdrawal rates that are sufficiently low to provide a high probability of success.

There are multiple assumptions behind the 4% rule that is important to be understood as they delve into the implications in the classic withdrawal rate studies since some estimates about sustainable spending provide a broadly optimistic outlook.

- The data available on hand does not help portray an image that is very accurate and can predict what the future might hold.

- Available data have not tested retirement spending that might be negatively affected by high stock market valuations and low-interest rates.

- Real-world investors' portfolios may underperform compared to the underlying tax returns.

- Risk increases as you move towards income investment approaching.

- Sustainable spending is reduced for a taxable portfolio by taxes.

- Building a safety margin at the end of the thirty-year timespan is desired.

- The period may exceed 30 years.

This chapter provides the details essential to the "probability-based" retirement planning school of thought. This is especially important for people who plan to fund their retirements with an investment portfolio and are wary of income annuities or other insurance products. The debate is also crucial for the safety-first approach because retirees will generally seek to fund some discretionary expenses from investments after allocating enough reliable income assets to cover the basics. Finally, retirees face a tradeoff regarding investment spending in retirement because spending more now increases the risk of needing to cut spending later.

Retirees must weigh the risks of spending too little and too much—that is, being too frugal.

William Bengen noticed that real-world volatility was not considered and claimed that average portfolio returns could be used to calculate the sustainable withdrawal rate. William's study, Journal of Financial Planning, "Determining Withdrawal Rates Using Historical Data," helped to bring about the modern area of retirement withdrawal rate research.

In this, he set up an example where a couple has retired and plans to take out an amount adjusted for inflation from their savings at the end of each year for thirty-five years. The couple's age of 65 would take the end of their retirement period to age 95. Bengen thought that this was a reasonable estimate.

He investigated the S&P index from a copy of Ibbotson Associates' Stocks, Bonds, Bills, and Inflation Yearbook. He used it to represent the stock market. Short-term government bonds are used, while intermediate-term government bonds represent the bond market.

He used a procedure called "historical simulations" to procure 30-year periods. He then used it to calculate the highest possible withdrawal rate for each of these simulations.

Let's assume that we start our retirement period with a $1 million portfolio. The SAFEMAX rate of 4.03 would mean that $40,300 can be withdrawn by us at the beginning of each year. In every year that follows, the amount can increase by the realized inflation rates. This process can be repeated for 30 years.

The 4% rule became the guideline for retirement withdrawals when he noticed that sequence-of-return risk would lower safe, sustainable withdrawal rates below what the average portfolio return over retirement implies.

High stock allocations support higher withdrawal rates, while lower stock allocations bring about lower SAFEMAXs. But Bengen endorsed 50-75 stocks because in all the cases except the worst-case scenario, the upside potential was much more significant with a higher stock allocation. Higher withdrawal rates could be used with higher stock allocations to allow you to leave behind more legacy at any given rate.

In early research, simplifying assumptions were used to provide a more realistic assessment of sustainable spending than was found when assuming a fixed average investment return. These studies grew with time as financial planners, and the press decided to use the 4 percent rule as an appropriate guideline. *The concept has been so widespread, and people are so misinformed that they do not consider the retirement horizon.*

The gist of the 4 percent rule is that retirees meet their objectives: meet their lifestyle spending goal, they are assumed to have the desire to spend smoothly but also carry an appetite for market volatility, they don't reduce their spending over time but take into consideration withdrawals in response to realized financial market returns and their withdrawals are fixed and are adjusted for inflation. This is meant to keep the failure rate low.

Internationally, *the 4% rate has proven itself to be a problem.* SAFEMAX fell below 3 in an array of countries. The rate would have only been sufficient in these countries to sustain retirees for three years. SAFEMAX failed in an array of countries, including Spain, Germany, France, and Austria. Overall, the rule worked only 68% of the time, and the withdrawal rate had to be lowered to 2.8% to have a success rate of 90% across the aggregated international data.

To achieve more significant long-term investment gain, total-return investing focuses on constructing diverse portfolios without the emotional roller-coaster of the downside market.

Bengen considered 30 years to be a considerable period for 65-year-olds retiring. Hence a method should be adopted that a horizon is selected that you are unlikely to live through and developing a plan that works that long. It goes without saying that the horizon should be greater than the average life expectancy. Those who decide to retire at a later stage in life might have to develop a shorter plan compared to those who retire at a younger age, who must establish a more extended plan. A longer plan would mean that the spending must be cut down to sustain the plan for longer.

Diversifying asset choice can help support a higher sustainable spending rate. It can even dial down the risk and return tradeoffs. So, if the expected portfolio return rate does not increase, the sustainable withdrawal rate could be adjusted if portfolio volatility is less.

Another way of supporting a higher withdrawal rate is placing a floor on the downside risk using a **Fixed Index Annuity.**

When discussing total-return rates, an assumption is made for the withdrawal rate studies that the asset allocation remains fixed throughout retirement and is adjusted to the targeted budget at the end of each year. In order to lower a portfolio's volatility at major points in retirement, changing asset allocation with a total-return investment portfolio can be understood. If market returns are historically good, retirees are still susceptible to bad returns in early retirement. Sequence risk can be lowered by fluctuating spending and reducing the portfolio's volatility.

Besides using a low-equity allocation through retirement (which has its risks) to reduce volatility, the rising glide path concept can be used when exposed to total wealth losses. In this, it aims to reduce the volatility in the most important around retirement, when a retiree has the most chance of losing the most dollar due to a market drop.

People are most susceptible when their wealth is at its peak. Thus, stock holdings are higher in its initial years, at their lowest around the retirement age, and higher as time passes. Contrary to common wisdom, which generally holds that stock allocation should decrease with age, the idea of a rising equity glide path in retirement defies logic. The growing equity glide route, on the other hand, is meant to be used as a risk-management strategy in retirement. It might boost retirement expenditure and wealth at a period when the aims of retirement might be most in danger.

Bengen defined the sustainable spending rate as the percentage of retirement-date assets that can be withdrawn, with the amount being adjusted for inflation in the years that follow. In this case, the portfolio does not run out for at least 30 years if at least 50% of the allocation belongs to stocks. Annual spending increases concurrently with the inflation rate of the previous year.

While this reflects what most retirees desire, to make their spending as smooth as possible, in the real world, they must adjust their spending over time adjusts to the performance of their portfolio and plan for the possibility of a market crash.

It is important to have room for flexibility because when a portfolio loses its value, the sequence of risk returns can be lowered by reducing spending from a volatile portfolio. However, an argument can be created that retirees who want to spend constantly should use a portfolio with lower volatility. Those who accept the portfolio's volatility should also accept spending volatility. Thus, sequence risk should be managed by letting the spending fluctuate with time.

The fixed percentage withdrawal strategy and constant inflation strategies are on opposite ends of the spectrum for spending strategies. The fixed percentage withdrawal strategies call for the retiree to spend a fixed amount in each year of retirement. On the other hand, a constant inflation-adjusted spending strategy calls for the retiree to spend an amount adjusted for inflation where the withdrawal rate will fluctuate with the portfolio value. But with a fixed percentage rule, the withdrawal rate stays the same while spending adjusts.

Fixed percentage strategy comes with its pros and cons. As a retiree is supposed to spend a percentage of what remains, the portfolio never runs out. The possibility of spending falling to very low levels still remain. But the concept of portfolio failure rates is inapplicable here. Additionally, the portfolio will grow if the market returns are higher than the spending rate.

We must identify the hidden cost of reducing spending today to protect our future and enjoy the highest standard of living available to us, risking making cutbacks later in life. Usually, withdrawal rate studies do not take into consideration what is lost in terms of one's satisfaction in life by spending less.

When considering a portfolio that is being taken out of its vacuum, we need to consider four interrelated factors: Reliable income sources, Longevity risk aversion, Spending flexibility, and availability of reserves. These factors dictate the acceptability of the probability of success. A plan with a high success rate may be necessary for someone who leans on backup reserves because of a lack of income.

But someone who does not fear living longer than his portfolio and has additional income sources might prefer a strategy with a higher spending rate but a lower probability of success. Some people might prefer a higher withdrawal rate as a part of downplaying the potential impact of investment portfolio depletion.

Buffer assets are assets that are separate from the portfolio and can be used in times when retirement spending fails to be sufficient. These assets should not depreciate with a general market downturn.

Chapter 4

Assessing Your Retirement Goals and Plans

Whether one is financially on the right track to having a successful retirement is a crucial question that many people who are nearing or have reached retirement ask themselves. This chapter offers a method for figuring out the response.

We try to assess whether there are enough assets to cover the anticipated retirement liabilities, including desirable reserves for spending shocks. We calculate the household's assets and liabilities to determine which is larger.

Let's begin by outlining how to put numbers on and quantify the financial objectives for retirement. These targets specify the costs or liabilities that must be covered and funded. It takes work to create a realistic retirement budget that accounts for spending during retirement to fulfill our ongoing requirements and wants. In order for the retiree to be completely certain that the plan can also manage expenditure shocks and other retirement risks, I typically estimate additional potential expenses for a variety of contingencies that the retiree would like to have on hand. I also take into account legacy aspirations, which can be expressed as excess wealth after enough assets have been set aside for ongoing expenses and unforeseen circumstances, or they can be explicitly included as an obligation to fund.

As we build the retirement balance sheet and eventually match assets with liabilities, I then turn towards assets. What options are there for managing retirement costs? We can identify the assets and liabilities and then calculate the funded ratio. This ratio of assets to liabilities assumes that future income and expenses will be expressed in terms of today's money using a conservative interest rate. If retirees only invest in low-risk assets to cover their lifetime liabilities, the funded ratio will tell us whether the plan will still be viable. Assets exceeding liabilities and having a funded status of greater than 100% is a fantastic outcome since it indicates readiness for retirement. I also think about what I might do if my retirement is not adequately funded, and my assets fall short of my liabilities.

The general retirement income issue I am aiming to resolve is laid out in the retirement income challenge. Developing a retirement income strategy entail identifying retirement goals, successfully achieving those goals, and safeguarding them against retirement hazards. To optimize the balance between these objectives in ways that complement our unique retirement income style, we must figure out how to best combine retirement income instruments and techniques. The retirement income challenge is depicted as a sequence of concentric rings in the figure below. The method for generating retirement income is summed up in the innermost circle. We must mix up different income streams to effectively accomplish goals and balance risks. The second circle has a list of potential objectives. The obstacles that those goals face is outlined in the third circle. The last circle displays the retirement income options.

Do you have enough assets to pay for the tools you'll need to manage your retirement risks and achieve your goals?

The Retirement Income Challenge

We start with the goals when tackling the retirement income challenge. The four Ls of retirement income include:

- **Lifestyle**
- **Longevity**
- **Legacy**
- **Liquidity**

We review how to measure these objectives, beginning with the retirement budget.

The main financial objective for the majority of retirees pertains to their annual spending: maximize spending power (*lifestyle*) to maintain spending in a stable and sustainable manner without any significant decreases, regardless of how long the retirement lasts (*longevity*). This is the budget for retirement. Other significant objectives may include leaving assets (*legacy*) for future generations and keeping adequate reserves for unforeseen events that have not been designated for other purposes (*liquidity*).

Setting the Retirement Budget

The main financial objective in retirement is to have enough money to cover your planned costs for the rest of your life. Although we won't immediately draw a line between longevity and lifestyle goals and the budget or spending plan, they are related. Although creating a budget is not always easy, there are tools that can make the process faster and easier. If budgeting gives you the assurance that you are on track, it might help you feel more confident and at peace about retiring.

When you have no idea how much you have been spending or how much you will maintain a happy lifestyle, it is normal to worry about whether you have enough money saved for retirement. Making a budget makes it simpler to gauge retirement preparation.

You might already have enough money saved up, which could be extremely reassuring. You can create a strategy for what to do if you are underfunded.

Delaying retirement, cutting back on planned expenses, or anticipating a greater rate of return on your assets seem to be other alternatives you can consider. This might even provide you with more clarity. Now, a large source of uncertainty may be managed and understood better.

Budgeting for retirement is challenging, though, because many expenses may shift when you start to retire. New retirees go through a substantial lifestyle change. Adjustments may be required to take into account changes occurring at retirement, even for those who have kept meticulous records of their annual spending over the years prior to retiring. This is particularly true for retirees who move as a part of their retirement. Budgeting for retirement is keeping track of your spending and making plans for how those expenses are expected to alter.

You will require a plausible estimation of the starting costs. *What do you predict will be your annual budget and spending once you retire? Will your overall retirement expenses increase slower or faster than the rate of inflation?*

Rate of Replacement

Budgeting for retirement is difficult, though, because many expenses may change once you retire. New retirees undergo a significant lifestyle transformation. Even for people who have kept detailed records of their annual spending in the years preceding retirement, adjustments may be required to account for changes that occur during retirement. This is especially true for retirees who move as part of their retirement. Budgeting for retirement is keeping track of your spending and planning for how those expenses are projected to change. You will need a reasonable estimate of the first costs. What do you expect your annual budget and spending to be once you retire? Will your overall retirement expenses rise slower or higher than inflation?

This is an average replacement rate, but this varies from individual to individual, case to case. When annual revenue fluctuates, the question becomes: **80% of what?**

This recommendation does not apply to early retirees who save more. It also overlooks early retirement splurging. Preretirement spending may include house payments and childcare that will no longer be needed. Those who saved, paid a mortgage, raised children, paid payroll taxes, and had certain job costs may be able to live comfortably on a substantially lower percentage of their preretirement earnings. It's not useful because simple planning can lead to more accurate retirement cost estimates.

Keeping Track of Recent Expenditures

Putting together a spending strategy for retirement is the best place to begin. In this regard, it will be beneficial to start by taking a look at real spending over the course of the last several years. Your spending habits may shift once you retire. Still, it's essential to have a precedent set or a round figure for comparison to identify all of the expenses that you usually wouldn't worry about.

Although the inflation rates had been quite low over the past few years, with the financial crisis upon us, things have changed and turned around considerably. As a result, you may want to change your historical costs to take into account rising prices and to make those expenses more reflective of the purchasing power that is available now. As soon as you have a general sense of your recent expenditures, it will be much simpler for you to adjust these numbers to account for the things that may change when you enter retirement.

Let's go ahead and think of a basic list of spending areas (needs and wants) that you should include in your budget. This list of general expense categories and subcategories can be used to construct a spreadsheet where you can fill in the relevant numbers. The spreadsheet can then be used to keep track of your spending. You are at liberty to modify these categories in whatever manner you deem appropriate.

You have the ability to reorganize your expenses, combine some of them into a single category, or add new ones as necessary for your circumstances. In addition, new categories could be introduced on an as-needed basis in order to accommodate particular circumstances that do not easily fall into any of these preexisting categories:

- **Clothing**
- **Charity**
- **Credit card rewards** (points for travel, cash back)
- **Debt repayments** (mortgage, vehicle loans, university loans, credit cards, and other debts)
- **Food** (groceries, eateries) (groceries, restaurants)
- **Health care** (insurance and Medicare premiums, out-of-pocket spending, dental, vision)
- **Home upkeep** (landscaping, snow removal, home security, pool, cleaning, pests, HVAC tune-up)

- **Recreation** (hobbies, leisure activities)
- **Gifts** (family support, education expenses)
- **Household costs** (rent, HOA dues, repairs)
- **Premiums for insurance** (home, vehicle, umbrella, life, disability, long-term care)
- **Memberships** (clubs, organizations, fitness, etc.)
- **Household miscellaneous expenses** (cleaning supplies, appliances, computers)
- **Self - care**
- **Phone** (cellular, landline)
- **Subscription services** (newspapers, magazines, software, internet, music, and cloud storage)
- **Taxes** (FICA, Medicare, state income, property, and local taxes)
- **Internet and television** (internet, cable TV, streaming services)
- **Transportation** (car repair, gas, parking, insurance, and roadside help)
- **Transportation** (flights, hotel, insurance, local transportation, and entry tickets)
- **Services** (water, electric, gas, home oil, waste disposal, sewage)
- **Significant outlays** (child's wedding, automotive purchase, significant house remodeling, a trip)

For example, only, a mortgage payment or property taxes could be placed in a general housing expense category, as debt repayment, or as taxes, depending on what makes the most sense to you. When it comes to mortgages, keep in mind that many mortgage payments include monies for property taxes and homeowner's insurance, which must be accounted for in the budget after the mortgage is paid off. Someone considering moving and renting in retirement may consider those fees as subsequently translating into rent.

Insurance is another broad category, with many of its costs likely appearing elsewhere instead. **For example,** homeowner's insurance could be classed as part of house expenses, auto insurance as part of transportation expenses, life insurance as a separate category, and medical-related insurance as part of health expenses.

Another issue may arise while shopping at large box stores that sell groceries as well as other things. Trying to separate expenses might be difficult. My answer, for example, is to list all Costco purchases as groceries, even though I know this is not the case. It is great to design a unique system that makes sense for you and helps to simplify your life if one is consistent and contains categories that record all spending. The most important factor is total overall spending.

When it comes to combining expenses, I find it easier to have a general home expense category where I combine things like clothing, entertainment, gifts, memberships, miscellaneous household expenses, personal care, and subscriptions, all of which were different categories above.

I think this works well for my family, and it is easier to keep track of fewer budget categories. My personal budget has the following categories: home repairs, HOA dues, cell phone, internet, TV, utilities, insurance (car, home, umbrella, disability), groceries, restaurants, household expenses, transportation, health care, travel, business deductions, education and camps for children, credit card rewards, life insurance premiums, charity, and taxes (federal income, FICA, Medicare, state income, local property).

Having established the categories for expenses, you are going to need some sort of method to track your costs. Credit cards offer the chance to simplify the process of budgeting for people who are able to manage the responsibility of not going over their spending limits while using credit cards. The statements that come with credit cards offer a transparent record of the money spent. Credit cards can also provide possibilities to earn points or cash back, which can be used to cut expenses. It's possible that those who have greater problems keeping their spending under control could benefit from using a debit card instead of a credit card because it also makes it possible to keep track of expenses, despite the fact that debit cards often don't come with rewards or other perks.

I once read that the rewards you get from credit card spending are more of an expense than an actual reward. I wholeheartedly agree with this, and so I treat these rewards as an expense too. This helps me keep my overall spending under control.

When it comes to cash back, this is an easy component to include. Incorporating the value of plane or hotel benefits received through rewards on credit cards can be meaningful, but it does require additional work. This is done to better estimate total travel expenses, especially if one is reducing those expenses by using points that may not always be available.

For example, only, if I use points to pay for a flight ticket that normally costs $550, I will save myself some money. I will generate a fictitious transaction with the costs associated with purchasing that aircraft ticket, and then I will generate a second fictitious transaction with the points as a negative monetary value that will cancel out the cost of the ticket. For the sake of my budget, this will increase the travel expense category; but my overall expenses will remain the same.

Classifying expenses when making cash purchases is a different problem. Personally, I don't carry or use cash. Keeping track of how the money is spent when using cash entails additional labor. Since I rarely use cash, I streamline this procedure by classifying all ATM withdrawals as regular household expenses at the time they are made.

My budget's breakdown by category is not significantly affected by this, and the total amount of expenses will remain accurate. It might be simple to monitor total expenses and prevent leakages with spending from other places by keeping track of expenditures from all bank accounts and credit cards.

Other minor adjustments might occasionally need to be made, for instance, if cash or a gift card is received that does not normally appear in online transaction reports. Additionally, you should review your pay stubs to ensure that taxes and the entire cost of any employment benefits that you would have to pay on your own after retiring are taken into consideration. Additionally, those costs would not typically appear on bank or credit card statements.

Some people may turn to budgeting in order to identify and cut down on unnecessary spending. When you look back through your past expenses, you may find recurring charges for services you are no longer using, which presents a chance to cancel such charges and reduce other unnecessary spending.

When dealing with situations like this, having categories that are more specific is helpful. For other people, the objective is limited to calculating their total annual expenditures. It's possible that you'll need fewer categories for your expenses, with the exception of having distinct categories for costs that will shift once you retire.

For instance, I have a separate area in my own budget for the costs associated with my children's education and summer camp, given that these kinds of expenditures can add up to a significant amount of money and will no longer be necessary once my children have reached adulthood. This category has the potential to expand into presents for grown children or grandchildren as well.

You also have the option of deciding how to handle the purchase of cars and other expensive things, as well as making house improvements that are an infrequent occurrence but nevertheless benefit the homeowner in the long run. Include purchases in the year in which they were made, then after that, figure out what the annual average spending is for that category. This is a straightforward approach.

This brings up another essential aspect, which is the fact that you should think about the costs of at least a few years' worth of living expenses in order to guarantee that you do not overlook any one-time high-priced purchases. When compared to a year in which such expenses were not incurred, looking at the average annual spending amount reveals a rise.

In this aspect, I find it more beneficial to think about budgeting on an annual basis rather than a monthly basis since monthly spending can vary by such a large amount for the same sorts of causes that cause annual expenses to fluctuate. There are other significant expenditures that may only materialize once or twice each year, such as annual premiums or property taxes. The problem of variable expenses tends to become less of a concern as the year progresses; nonetheless, it is still vital to be aware of the times of the year when significant expenditures are expected to be incurred in order to ensure that sufficient money is available. Additionally, if you have identified significant one-time expenses for retirement, such as a house renovation or the wedding of a child, you may want to monitor these as separate obligations outside of your budget.

I've included some examples of my own budgeting, which may assist in understanding how I do it. I like to keep a spreadsheet where I can track my annual expenditures. I like to change categories in my spreadsheet using the raw downloaded numbers. I reclassify several spending categories because online options don't follow the exact categories that I like for my costs to be split in.

I also exclude credit card bill payments and savings transfers because they reflect duplicate counting or items that are not truly expenses (unless you pay interest on your credit cards). I try to update my spending spreadsheet at least once a quarter because occasionally, I need to recall how particular expenses should be categorized, and waiting too long can make that difficult. Payments made by check are likewise classified correctly, and as previously stated, ATM withdrawals are classified as ordinary household expenses. This gives me an excellent record of annual spending that I can continue to expand on and follow over time.

Chapter 5

Bucketing

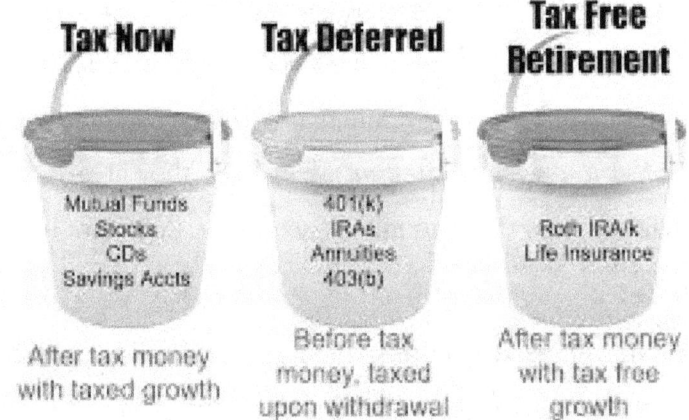

THREE TAX BUCKETS

Tax Now   **Tax Deferred**   **Tax Free Retirement**

Mutual Funds
Stocks
CDs
Savings Accts

401(k)
IRAs
Annuities
403(b)

Roth IRA/k
Life Insurance

After tax money with taxed growth

Before tax money, taxed upon withdrawal

After tax money with tax free growth

Bucketing is a retirement option plan. This is where you put money into an individual retirement account.

Bucketing is a smart option to catalog your portfolio. Let's look at it this way: there are three different buckets. All of them carry different levels of risk and investment based on different factors. These include your goals, need for funds, risk tolerance, and the time frame required.

This will vary depending mostly on your financial standing (*where you are currently*) and your financial goals (where *you plan to go*). Of course, these numbers will change when you move closer to retirement, and you should revisit this on an annual basis.

Inside the Three Buckets

Let us take a deeper look inside these buckets:

Bucket 1

The first bucket is for immediate cash requirements. These resources won't increase dramatically (*it can be said that it is similar to a savings account*). However, they are available right away if money is needed on an urgent basis.

Bucket 2

The initial stage of your retirement requirements is catered for in the second bucket. The idea behind this bucket is to make it easily available whenever you need it. This may be for your "red zone" retirement years, during which you may be consulting, working on a contractual basis, or freelancing. To counteract inflation and provide money in the form of dividends or interest, it should progressively increase over time.

Bucket 3

The third bucket comes into play in the later stage of your retirement. It covers assets that you plan on leaving behind in your will for family members or charity.

For the purpose of beating the impact of inflation, these assets are geared toward long-term growth.

Establishing Your Buckets

The first step in preparing for planned retirement is understanding how and when you should fill your buckets. This can be divided and categorized into four investment stages: accumulation, transition, preservation, and distribution. The greater amount of funds you can devote to buckets two and three, the longer you have to attain your objectives. However, the numbers may fluctuate as you move closer to retirement based on timelines and the required amount of funds.

To get you through the collection and accumulation years, whether it's for college fees or home repairs, bucket number one is often a small proportion of the portfolio assets. However, five to fifteen years after retirement, the transition period begins. You should start transferring more from bucket three to bucket two during this period. When you are five years away from retirement, you should increase your investment in bucket one while extending the transition from bucket three to bucket two. To avoid market exposure as you approach retirement, you should have a lesser amount in bucket three.

Typically, these bucket portfolios comprise taxable, tax-deferred, and tax-free investments. Usually, buckets two and three take full advantage of these tax benefits, particularly throughout the accumulating and transitioning stages.

Risk Response

When it comes to finances, there is always a risk. Considering how the market and economy are so volatile these days, it is best to come up with back up plans. Investors may have a hard time accepting the necessity to lower risk in their portfolios. A perfect example for this can be the extraordinarily long bull market until 2022. As a result, moving their money, for instance, from bucket three to bucket two (and bucket one, in rare situations) was seen as a tough choice. In the past, this has proved tricky due to low-interest rates and returns, but the risk is that the market may continue to collapse further. Comparatively to investors who were more diligent about the bucketing process, individuals who didn't reallocate their assets and plan to retire in the next two to three years are witnessing a considerable loss in their portfolios.

It's crucial to regularly review your allocations, especially during times of market volatility or a downturn. By relocating their profits closer to safer assets as they approach their retirement goals, investors who were fortunate enough to have good returns in bucket three could safeguard their earnings. If not, it could be too late to transition.

What happens when they can't afford it is that they take on too much risk. That can entail putting off retiring earlier or working more hours. *You always want to make sure you have a portion of your assets that will never lose money due to a downed market, make sure you always utilize buckets two and three correctly and make sure you have you can't outlive your retirement portfolio.*

Allocation and Distribution

I normally advise that you have 12 to 18 months' worth of estimated distribution in bucket one when you transition into distribution. The possible market volatility can then be absorbed by bucket number three. To keep bucket one filled, bucket two will also contribute any profits or interest it earns. This lowers the prospect of loss - especially on bad market days, market crashes, or during periods of depression. This, in terms, helps ensure that you can continue providing the level of income that was expected. While it may be true from a return standpoint that the assets in bucket one are not making a difference, the approach enables the other buckets to absorb market fluctuations without having an immediate negative impact on cash needs. Because of inflation and market factors, cash as an asset class may underperform in the long run. However, it must be noted that it does offer support and stability when the market conditions are volatile.

Dealing with the Impacts of a Bull Market

Things have considerably changed and evolved with time. The days of relying solely on bond interest and investment dividends for monthly income are long gone. Since the 2008 Market Crash, bonds have considerably lagged behind and are no longer the suitable choice for investor portfolios.

People's expectations of the amount of money they will have when they retire have changed as a result of this. Some people have taken on more risk and gone for payouts they might not have earlier. Because of this, they may have a little bit more in buckets two and three than is traditionally thought appropriate given their planned retirement date.

Since the market has been growing, many investors have become overly confident. In their 401(k)s, they managed to overlook guaranteed and stable value funds. As a result, a large number of younger generations are adopting IULs and other forms of life insurance as a retirement planning and adding extra protection, while the 35+ generation is adding life insurance, IULs, and transferring funds from their 401(k)s to annuities as they near retirement. With IULs and Annuities featuring a stop loss where, according to the contract, you cannot lose money, an increasing number of people are adopting this as a retirement guarantee bucket in addition to a 401(k).

There are many steps you may take to safeguard investments while still enjoying your present lifestyle if you are close to retirement but still require additional income.

A few of these steps include:

- Think of consulting or freelancing for a few years for extra funds that can go into your retirement account.

- See if working from home is an option. Going remote will reduce expenses for commute and travel while also saving you extra time. These are some money-saving techniques that may help in the long term.
- Evaluate the risk your portfolio poses to a long-term care plan and decide if you should finance an LTC coverage while you are still employed or add an annuity with an LTC built in.
- Get a jumpstart start on your retirement plans by saving money through downsizing current housing.
- Invest in other income options, such as renting out property.
- If you're an entrepreneur, look at ways you can increase your cash flow and reduce your losses. Also, consider whatever tax-saving ideas you may have. These will make your retirement easier.

With generally low-interest rates and a volatile market, it's necessary to get creative with your assets in a way that might not correlate to the broader market.

The Next Steps that Come Before Retirement

Examine your portfolio and figure out the amount you need for every bucket if you are close to retiring and feel pressured by the global economic downturn. You will need to thoughtfully develop and execute a bucket strategy in order to successfully navigate the market, plan for your retirement, and ensure you have sufficient funds for the transition period.

Here are a few pointers that will help considerably:

- Every year, evaluate your cash requirements and reallocate to the proper buckets.

- Keep your bucket percentages in check and rebalance as necessary, especially when the markets are rising and you can lock in profits.

- Examine the amount of revenue coming in from your second bucket each year. Deposit money in bucket one just as you are now doing, or reinvest it for potential future profits.

- If you plan to take distributions, allocate money for up to 2 years in bucket one.

- Regularly evaluate the items in buckets two and three. Knowing where your funds are being invested will allow you to make adjustments according to your needs and market trends. Make sure you have a no-loss investment as part of your portfolio. The sooner you start, the better.

- Perform yearly tax predictions to find an appropriate balance between taxable and tax-deferred accounts, allowing you to withdraw money while still paying taxes at a manageable rate.

Be mindful of moving your portfolio to any of these buckets in case the markets rally. It could be alluring to adopt a "fear of losing out" mentality and aim for high payouts. But use restraint. Pruning holdings that might not be the best candidates for recovery and positioning those assets for potentially better alternatives will help you remove emotion from investing.

Living without concern, without having to check your emails and attend meetings, or feeling anxious about the status of your portfolio is the best aspect of retirement. Utilizing a bucketing technique and practicing discipline will allow you to make sure you have enough money to make the most of your retirement.

There are plenty of options that you can look into. These include:

- 401k – Goes up and down with the market – Not risk-free.

- IRA – ROTH – Goes up and down with the market – Not risk-free.

- Life Insurance – Guarantee not to lose money – **Risk-free.**

- Social Security – Guarantee not to lose money – **Risk-free.**

- Fixed Index Annuities – Guarantee not to lose money – **Risk-free.**

- Stocks – Goes up and down with the market – Not risk-free.

- Pension Plans – Guarantee not to lose money – **Risk-free.**

Ensure that there are no losses in your retirement fund. The returns are typically not as large, but you do not lose money when the market falls. Including this in your retirement plan ensures that you will never outlive your retirement savings. Having a good mix is an ideal plan for retirement. Never put all your assets in one bucket.

Chapter 6

(FIA) Fixed Index Annuities as Your Retirement Plan

You can use fixed index annuities to save money for retirement and to ensure a steady monthly income after you retire; basically, a retirement plan. If you want the chance to receive indexed interest but are unwilling to gamble your money and lose it in the market, Fixed Index Annuity can be a smart option for you to consider. Additionally, it also offers certain tax benefits since it is created to assist you with your financial planning post-retirement.

It is becoming more common for those who are preparing for retirement to use annuities, particularly fixed index annuities. Fixed index annuities combine the appealing qualities of other forms of annuities while attempting to deal with the less desirable aspects.

Think of it this way, adding another Social Security to your retirement plan. A Social Security check is a life annuity.

With a life annuity, the period of time for increasing payments is the rest of your life, no matter how long you live. Your Social Security check will not stop until you die.

How does FIA Work?

The two stages of Fixed Index Annuities include the accumulation and distribution periods. During the accumulation period, you are allowed to accrue wealth and grow it. This is where your annuities grow, and you don't have to worry about paying taxes over them, either.

Stage 1: Accumulation

1. Buy a Fixed Index Annuity: This is a simple contract between you and an insurance provider is an annuity. You make a purchase payment (or premium) to the insurance company. In return, you receive advantages that your annuity contract with the insurance provider guarantees.

2. Annuity earns Interest: Your annuity may generate "indexed interest." This is also known as interest based on the growth of an external index throughout the accumulation phase. However, the money in your annuity is not at stake because you are not actively

trading. Instead, **you can earn an interest rate guaranteed by insurance and fixed annually.**

3. Your annuity grows tax-deferred: Until you withdraw money from your annuity, you are not required to pay taxes on the interest your contract produces. As a result, the money in your annuity may accrue more quickly due to the tax deferral.

Stage 2: Distribution

1. Annuity becomes Income: You may then receive the amount permitted by your FIA (Fixed Index Annuity) contract in a lump payment, over a predetermined time, or as income for the remainder of your life after the time period stated by your contract. Sometimes, annuities may even offer the chance to increase revenue.

Why Should Retirees Consider Fixed Index Annuities?

1. Your agreement with a life insurance provider is called a Fixed Index Annuity (FIA). With this contract, you give the insurance company a premium in exchange for monthly income payments made

over time, starting at a certain time in the future. **Fixed index annuities are becoming increasingly important to new retirees due to rising life expectancies, declining incomes, market loss, avoiding probate, and payouts that you can't outlive, just to name a few.**

A Fixed Index Annuity can help you with the following:

- Have tax-deferred growth.
- Principal protection.
- Create a large retirement income, something you can't outlive.
- Help you create and leave behind a legacy.
- Tax-deferred growth.
- Has no contribution restrictions.
- Quickly transfer money at the time of death/upon death.
- Avoid ending up in probate.
- Prevents market losses when the market crashes.

More on the Benefits of FIA

Stock Market Loss Elimination

Fixed Index Annuities give a chance to profit from stock market gains. Your money, less any relevant costs, may be able to earn income when you buy an FIA based on changes in an external index, such as the S&P 500 or Nasdaq-100. You take advantage of the chance to invest in the market increase. Conversely, your contract's value stays the same if equities decline.

Principal Protection

The insurance provider fully guarantees and protects your capital and accumulated interest from stock market losses.

As a result, your premium value and all accrued interest are both guaranteed to remain intact.

Tax Deferred Growth

Your contributions' interest accrual is tax-free, and you only pay taxes on it when you take the money. *Additionally, when you use an annuity's proceeds to pay for long-term care insurance, you are no longer required to pay federal income tax on those proceeds. Even if services aren't used, money made to insurance companies under standard long-term care insurance policies is forfeited.* However, unused duties in an annuity are the sole property of the account holder and may one day be taken. Additionally, because there are fewer requirements to meet, receiving coverage through a long-term care annuity may be simpler if you are too sick or unwell to qualify for a standard long-term care insurance policy.

Income You Can't Outlive

You can start getting payouts from your annuity after a predetermined amount of time has passed. There are several products with features that let the income increase with inflation. Depending on how the annuities are set up, they may also offer benefits besides the guaranteed periodic payments, such as emergency funds for when they are required, death benefits, nursing home benefits, and lifetime income benefits, **which ensure that the annuity's holder won't ever outlive the income it provides.**

Provide a Legacy with Death Benefits

You should think about the financial impact this could have on your family if you have a longer life expectancy. Most of us will wish to leave our heirs a legacy. **Leftover funds can be transferred to recipients tax-free through the death benefit of fixed index annuities.**

The Difference Between Fixed Index Annuity and Other Plans: Why Should One Choose FIA?

In contrast to 401(k)s and IRAs, you can contribute an unlimited amount to your annuity, and the growth is tax-deferred (there are no IRS limits on the amount of money you can contribute to an annuity). You can start withdrawing from an income source depending on the contract's accumulation value after a predetermined amount of time (as soon as 12 months or sooner depending on the annuity and the contract). The accumulation value is equal to the whole premium you paid plus 100% interest earned less any withdrawals, surrender fees, unpaid loans you took upon your principal, and fees for any optional riders you might have chosen. Not all annuities have fees, and some don't have any fees at all. Fixed index annuities offer bonds' fixed income features, although they are unaffected by fluctuations in interest rates. Additionally, they provide gains independent of equities market losses as the equity market increases or decreases.

Making Fixed Index Annuities a Part of Your Retirement Plan

If you're searching for a retirement investing strategy that safeguards your principal, has some solid upside potential, and offers predictable, guaranteed lifelong investment returns in retirement, FIA may be an option. In fact, it may be the best option for you.

If you're planning to retire and are worried about what happens next, this is the right book for you. We will go through the many retirement possibilities, strategies, things you should know, the dos and don'ts, things to watch out for, some things to remember and keep in mind, dangers and risks, and much more.

The number one goal for smart retirement planning is knowing and appreciating money and its importance. Understand that you spent all your life earning that money, and so you simply cannot afford to lose it so soon. Invest it wisely; so that it serves a greater purpose for you later on in life when you really need it. The closer you get to retirement, the greater importance you must place on a safe investment. 401(k)s, and IRAs have a place in retirement, but they **SHOULD NOT** be your only source of retirement income. You need a component of your retirement savings that you cannot outlive or lose.

Chapter 7

FIA Benefits

Contract Value Growth

Since FIAs are fixed annuities, the returns that emerge from their contract value are termed "crediting interest." FIA premiums are added to the insurance company's general account, and the owner receives interest based on a fixed rate or the performance of a linked market index. FIAs offer interest that is tied to an index, but the money is not put directly into the index. There are no subaccounts. They just pay the owner interest based on a formula tied to the performance of the index.

FIAs can better manage downside and upside exposures with credited interest. FIAs safeguard the principal by crediting 0% interest even if the index drops dramatically. FIA owners will only receive a share of index profits to protect themselves. Unlike variable annuities, FIAs may reduce contract value volatility.

Insurance companies usually let you choose between different index options and a fixed interest option for FIAs.

Most of the time, people who own contracts can mix and match these options in any way they want, and they can change how these options are used at the start of each new term. The S&P 500 is a common choice for US stocks with a large market capitalization, and the MSCI EAFE index is a common choice for international stocks. With these indices, only the price returns (capital gains or losses) matter since dividends aren't taken into account when figuring out how much interest to give. This is because financial derivatives are used to link performance instead of owning the underlying assets, so dividends are not available.

There are a lot of different ways to give credit, and the trend is for those ways to get more complicated. With the chosen index, interest will usually be credited based on a formula that can include floors, caps, participation rates, and spreads. As an example, we'll look at a point-to-point crediting method with a participation rate and a one-year term that resets every year.

Interest will be determined based on the percentage change in the index from the beginning of the contract to the end, as well as the point-to-point nature of the one-year period. The annual point-to-point method compares the value of an index at two points in time that are separated by exactly one year. Interest is calculated based on the index gain for the year (the price return without dividends) and credited on the contract anniversary date following the end of each annual term. *Upside profits are credited based on a participation rate, with a zero percent floor guaranteeing no losses.*

The interest credited is calculated again at the beginning of each term, which is represented by the yearly reset structure. If the index fell 10% last year, but the FIA awarded no interest for that period, then all that matters for determining the interest due this term is the point-to-point decrease for this year. Because of the annual reset provision, future profits don't have to compensate for past losses.

The insurance company purchases sufficient bonds with the annuity contract value so that the growth of that portion, along with interest, will match the original contract value at the end of the term. This is one way to think about the downside protection that comes with the guaranteed floor. Another way to think about it is as follows: The "options budget" is the amount of money that is left over after the purchase of bonds to safeguard the principle. The insurance firm maintains a portion of this money in order to meet corporate expenses and profit objectives. The remaining money is used to purchase upside exposure to the index.

When the FIA gives a participation rate on the upside, the insurance firm has the ability to utilize the "options budget" to buy a one-year at-the-money call option on the S&P 500 index. This can happen whenever the FIA offers the participation rate. This is a type of financial derivative that confers the right, but not the responsibility, on its owner to purchase shares of the S&P 500 index at a predetermined price known as the option's strike price. If the option's strike price is equal to the index's current value, then the option is considered to be "at the money." If the value of the index drops during the term of the option, the option will expire worthless, but the bonds will still cover the principal. The owner of the call option will obtain exposure to the upside in the event that the index experiences capital gains throughout the term of the option. This does not include dividends that are reinvested. The participation rate is calculated by dividing the "options budget" by the price of the call option. This gives the percentage of index profits that are actually obtained.

The level of interest rates and the price of financial derivatives for the related index will have a major impact on establishing the parameters that an FIA will make available to its users. If the interest rate is high enough, the principal can be safeguarded with a smaller pool of assets. This frees up more money that can be allocated to the options budget, which can then be used to buy upside exposure. Less expensive call options will make it possible to purchase more upside participation and vice versa. A reduction in the implied volatility of the underlying index, a rise in the strike price of the option in relation to the current price of the index, a lower risk-free interest rate, and a shorter term to maturity are all factors that contribute to a decrease in the price of the options. If interest rates are sufficiently high and the cost of call options is low enough, it is possible that participation rates could be higher than one hundred percent. On a related note, it should be made abundantly clear that if the owner is willing to accept a lower floor, it would be possible to gain more upside potential because less would be required for bonds, and more would be available to purchase call options.

Furthermore, it's important to know that the amount of upside potential an FIA can offer will change over time as interest rates and the prices of call options change. With an annual reset design, the insurance company must have to do the same thing every year and will have to deal with different interest rates and prices for call options as these variables change over time. When interest rates rise, and call options are cheap, there's greater upside potential and vice versa.

With an indexed annuity, the floor could be negative, or there could be other ways for the contract value to go down. If the floor is less than zero, the annuity is technically a variable annuity. It has most of the same features as an FIA, but it is also regulated as a security because it can lose money. Structured annuities like these are becoming more popular and have different names, such as registered index-linked annuities. These annuities may also have buffers in addition to a negative floor.

For example only, if a product has a 10 percent buffer, it means that if the index goes down by up to 10%, the interest credited is 0%. If the index loses more than 10%, this method will give credit for the amount by which it lost more than 10%. A loss of 18% on the index would mean a loss of 8% on the annuity, but a loss of 8% on the index would mean no loss. By accepting this higher downside risk, there is more upside potential, which is one reason why they are becoming more popular in the market.

Lifetime Income Benefits

We just went over how the value of a deferred annuity contract might increase over time. To estimate a benefit base and guaranteed income amount for deferred annuities that provide lifetime withdrawal benefits, two distinct but parallel sets of computations may be used. We need to think about how the growth during the deferral and distribution periods is assured to provide revenue.

A lifetime income rider is not the same as annuitizing the contract in order to secure a guaranteed income, and this must be emphasized before proceeding. Even after lifetime payments begin, the contract is still in a deferred state. For the rest of the annuitant's life or the lives of both annuitants, if the contract was purchased jointly, the benefit rider will continue to support a specified yearly distribution amount. In the end, retirees are spending their own money, even while the underlying contract value of assets is still positive. After the value of the contract has been depleted, the insurance company will make payments out of its own funds. Once the value of the contract has been depleted, annuitization will occur.

Before beginning distributions, there is a period known as the accumulation period or the deferral period. At this time, you should first think about the growth process for the guaranteed benefit base. This increase is essential because it is eventually used to calculate the amount of income that is guaranteed to be delivered by the annuity over the beneficiary's lifetime. If the retirees begin taking lifetime distributions right away, they can avoid having to wait out the deferral period.

Lifetime income benefits can grow in two ways before they start. A benefit base, roll-up rate, and step-ups are used in the first technique. Deferred annuities with income guarantee riders allow you to lock in a guaranteed growth rate on the benefit base during the accumulation period and define the benefit base as the high watermark of the contract value of the underlying assets on anniversary dates if that growth is higher than the guaranteed rate. During withdrawal, the benefit base is used to compute guaranteed income. It differs from the contract value of assets, which the owner could access based on actual account growth net of fees and surrender charges.

With this strategy, one can secure a steady stream of income for the rest of their lives by taking a predetermined percentage of their guaranteed benefit base each year, beginning at a specified age. As with the annuity's initial contract value, this is equal to the premium paid into the annuity. The value of a contract's underlying assets can increase or decrease over time based on the level of investment returns actually earned and the amount and timing of any dividends or fees deducted from the underlying assets. If the value of the underlying assets in the contract reaches a new high watermark and is greater than the guaranteed benefit base on any anniversary, the guaranteed benefit base will be increased to reflect the new high watermark value. Guaranteed income after this point is higher as a result. If the value of the underlying contracted assets hasn't grown higher on its own during the deferral period before distributions begin, an annuity may offer a guaranteed roll-up rate to increase the benefit base automatically over time. In most cases, the higher guaranteed roll-up rate or the maximum increase in contract value is used to increase the benefit base.

It's common for people to mistake roll-up rates for guaranteed annuity returns. The contractual value of assets is unaffected by these rates. They are only responsible for establishing the hypothetical benefit base that will be used in conjunction with a guaranteed withdrawal rate to calculate the guaranteed lifetime income. What really counts is how these two elements work together.

The owner may start lifetime payouts at some point. Even if the account balance drops to zero, the retiree's guaranteed withdrawals never decrease. One example is that some companies offer a feature that allows for higher distributions when assets remain and smaller distributions once assets diminish. The owner can terminate the contract at any time and get the contract value of the remaining assets, net of surrender charges.

One-time distributions are not protected by the lifetime income guarantee rider in deferred annuities. Non-lifetime distributions are allowed before guaranteed income begins. That distinction is crucial since rollups usually terminate when assured distributions start. Thus, it allows them to continue. Non-lifetime distributions exceeding the guaranteed level are permissible after the guaranteed distributions begin, but they lower subsequent guarantees.

Once guaranteed lifetime distributions start, the end of the deferral period and the start of the distribution period. A guaranteed withdrawal or payout percentage rate based on age will be added to the value of the benefit base to figure out the guaranteed income. When you multiply the guaranteed withdrawal rate by the benefit base, you get a guaranteed distribution amount that endures throughout its life, even if the contract value of the assets is gone. Step-ups may even cause guaranteed distributions to go up if the underlying asset base hits new high watermarks on the dates when this is checked.

For example only, a company might offer the following payout rates to single people based on the age at which they can start taking money out: 4.5 percent for people aged 59 to 64, 5% for those aged 65 to 69, 5.5 percent for those aged 70 to 79, and 6.5 percent for those aged 80 and up. For couples, payout rates would usually be 0.5 percent lower and would be based on the age of the younger person. For couples, another possibility is that the payout rates are the same as for singles, but a higher fee is charged to support the guarantee over the longer expected joint lifetime. Most GLWB annuity payouts are the same for both men and women, which would help women, who tend to live longer than men.

Aside from the hypothetical benefit base and the rollup rate, there is another way to set up lifetime income benefits.

Variable annuities are more likely to use the method just described, while FIAs are more likely to use this other method. In the other method, when the GLWB is added to the annuity, a lifetime withdrawal percentage is set. This percentage is still based on age bands. In this case, the age at which the benefit is bought is more important than the age at which income starts. Then, instead of using a rollup rate with a benefit base, a deferral credit increases the withdrawal rate for each year that the owner delays the start of their lifetime income distributions. When lifetime distributions start, they are set as a percentage of the value of the contract at that time. Because of deferral credits, the percentage goes up over time.

For example only, let's say a 55-year-old person buys an FIA with this kind of income rider. When this contract is bought at age 55, the withdrawal percentage is 4.5%, and the deferral credit is 0.3% for each year that the person waits to start getting money. The person plans to retire at 65, which would be ten years later than if they retired at 65. That means that the percentage of the contract's value that can be taken out over a lifetime is 7.5% (4.5 + 0.3 x 10) at that age. In this case, only the gross amount of principal is protected before the rider fee is added at the end of every year

Many people mistake the guaranteed growth rate on their benefit base for a guaranteed investment return. They don't realize that the guaranteed income is based on the combination of the growth rate on the benefit base and the withdrawal rate applied to the benefit base. These two factors cannot be separated. When a higher roll-up rate is combined with a lower payout rate, it doesn't mean that the consumer is in a better position. For these reasons, the second deferral credit method is easier to understand and has a more direct relationship to how the payout rate of a deferred income annuity goes up with the length of deferrals.

The practical effect of the optional rider cost will be to erode the contract value a bit more quickly, resulting in a lower death benefit than otherwise. The rider fee is of secondary relevance, given the emphasis on revenue rather than accumulation. The objective is not to discover the annuity with the lowest rider cost, as this would typically support a less generous guarantee, but rather to find the annuity that provides the greatest lifetime income value for a given rider cost. When the individual lives long enough for the annuity contract value to be depleted, the benefit continues to provide a lifelong income, and the earlier fee drag becomes immaterial.

Income riders on deferred annuities give you a chance to get "mortality credits," which can lower the number of assets you need to support a lifetime spending goal. *The rider fees paid for the income guarantee protect the spending in case the person lives too long or the market returns are so bad that they outlive their investment assets and can't get an income any other w*

Chapter 8

Important Documents of Legacy Planning

This chapter covers end-of-life planning as part of retirement income planning. First, we organize finances and prepare for retirement. This will benefit you, but we discuss it here to aid your loved ones. You'll understand how your funds connect together. Your financial affairs will also be in one spot for emergency use. When a family's financial manager dies or becomes incapacitated, difficulties occur. This prepares family members to lead.

We must discuss preparing your family for household money. To make these transitions as seamless as possible, take time to develop instructions and explanations and gather the necessary documents. This includes organizing your family and personal information, professional and service provider contact information, insurance information, medical history, and financial account and asset information.

Estate planning comes after organizing. Asset tracking starts estate planning. Check asset titles and beneficiary designations. Asset titles and beneficiary choices always outweigh a will. Yet, a will specifies how you want your property distributed after death. Consider a trust for estate management when making a will. Choosing a financial power of attorney and advance health care directives for incapacity management are further estate planning considerations.

So, if you can't, who makes medical and financial decisions?

One could also want to offer their final wishes, which might include things like burial preparations, names of people who ought to be contacted, notes to family and friends, advice for them, and other such things.

Be sure to have a conversation about the duties and obligations that come with the various powers and functions you assign to the people who will be required to step into those roles in the case of your passing or incapacity. You can make things simpler for everyone involved if you try to ensure that your desires are understood and if you attempt to achieve consensus and acceptance over your decisions. Because it will save them numerous hours of additional effort during already difficult occasions, your family will be grateful to you for keeping everything pre-planned and arranged in advance.

After our discussion of these preparations, we will continue our conversation about tax-efficiency and tax advantages as they apply to legacies. In the chapter before this one, we talked about tax planning, and one of the topics that we covered was how to maximize the effectiveness of retirement spending after taxes, so that you may maintain your spending goal for as long as feasible. It is only natural that a higher level of tax efficiency will be connected with the provision of a larger legacy. This is because there is a reduced likelihood of depleting all available resources in the process of mitigating the risk of living to an advanced age.

This chapter continues by explaining how decisions may change if supporting a legacy goal is an explicit part of retirement planning, or as it becomes clear that a retiree will not be spending all available assets, and there will be a legacy to coordinate. Alternatively, this chapter explains how decisions may change once it becomes clear that a retiree will not be spending all available assets. Tax planning for legacies should involve changes to withdrawal ordering decisions, the management of estate taxes, and an awareness of the required minimum distribution rules for a variety of tax-deferred assets that have been inherited. Although estate taxes are a possibility, most families won't have to worry about paying them because the exemptions are so high. Despite this, the rules governing estate taxes could shift at some point in the future, and the following chapter will present a few ideas that should be discussed with estate planning professionals.

After reading this chapter, it is my hope that you will be better equipped to grasp the choices available to you and to make the decisions that are necessarily planning your retirement with a professional.

Getting Your Financial House in Order

It is crucial, not only for you but also for those who depend on you, to get your financial affairs in order. It is also necessary for the event that you become dependent on other people as a consequence of a decline in brain function or any other impairments or illnesses. It is essential for all members of the family to be aware of the situation and be aware of what has to be done.

For instance, it would be pointless to pay payments for life insurance if no one was aware of the coverage after your passing. Since then, the money would be wasted. This section provides a synopsis for a subject that has been the subject of entire books' worth of writing in a summarized manner. While I will attempt to provide a summary of what you need to take into consideration, you can always contact us for further assistance.

Personal Information, Family History, and Financial Information

The first step is to compile all of your essential personal information and documents and then file them away in a location that is both secure and easily accessible. The following are some examples of personal objects that fall within this category:

- Birth Certificates
- Passports
- Social Security cards
- Driver's license
- Marriage license
- Prenuptial agreement

- Divorce documentation
- Adoption papers
- Immigration or citizenship documents
- Military Service Records
- Health insurance cards

In addition, you should place the task of organizing your emergency contacts and vital medical information extremely towards the top of your list of things to do in terms of priority. In the event of an emergency, who needs to be notified, and what information needs to be easily accessible, etc.? Key considerations include:

Emergency Contacts

Information to get in touch with close friends and neighbors (in case of emergency)

Contact information for the children – their schools etc. if they are attending.

Employer details: who to speak with at your place of employment, the availability of paid holidays off, and the various perks offered by your workplace.

Medical and health information: This comprises a list of all medications currently being taken and the appropriate dosages, any allergies, blood type, immunization records, doctors and physicians, and medical history.

Pets: information on how to get in touch with a veterinarian and specifics regarding who should take care of them

Most people have several financial and medical professionals with whom they collaborate, and it may be necessary to get in touch with some of them. It is essential to supply the names and relevant contact information for any of the following professionals:

- Financial advisor
- Attorney
- Estate plan attorney
- Insurance agent
- Banker
- Accountant
- Trust officer
- Executor
- Guardian
- Power of attorney for finance
- Power of attorney for healthcare
- Family physicians and other relevant medical professionals

Some of this information, such as names and phone numbers of people to call in an emergency and your medical history, should also be stored in your wallet and be carried at all times. If we are talking about the things that you might carry with you, it is a good idea to have a separate list of any credit cards or other stuff that might be in there. This may come in handy in the case that these items are misplaced or stolen.

Assets and Liabilities

Next, we explain how to access the household's net worth statement accounts. This information should include account titles and beneficiary designations. Bank account titling entails knowing ownership, access, and what happens if the person dies or becomes incapacitated. Bank accounts may have an ATM card and pin numbers to track. Your estate plan should also include instructions for handling assets and obligations.

This is a very detailed list that can include the following:

- Bank accounts - checking, savings, money market, CDs
- Credit union accounts

- Savings bonds (series, denomination, serial number, issue date)
- Treasury Direct account
- Brokerage accounts
- IRAs, Roth IRAs, and other individual retirement plans
- 401(k), 403(b), and employer-based qualified retirement plans
- Social Security statement and benefits
- Executive deferred compensation or other benefits
- Pensions
- Annuities
- Life Insurance
- Veteran benefits
- Workers' compensation
- Business interests, stock options, contracts
- Royalties, copyrights, trademarks, patents
- Education savings accounts (529 plans)
- ABLE accounts for children and young adults with disabilities
- Health Insurance – Group Insurance, Medicare etc.
- Supplement Insurance – Cancer, Heart-Attack, Stroke, Home HealthCare etc.

- Health Savings Accounts
- Real estate: home, second residences or vacation homes, timeshares, investment properties, farmland, etc.
- Real estate rental contracts related to long-term care, such as an assisted living facility or continuing care retirement community.
- Vehicles, including cars, trucks, boats, planes, RVs, etc.
- Uncollected legal judgments
- Other property you expect to receive from others.
- Collectibles inventory, including receipts and appraisals.
- Significant special possessions with documentation including photos or video recordings.
- Jewelry, antiques, artwork
- Reward and loyalty programs: credit cards, airlines, hotels, rental cars, etc.
- Storage units
- Digital assets: email, eBooks, music, videos, blogs, LinkedIn, Twitter, etc.
- Crypto-currency accounts

Meanwhile, liabilities related to debt holdings include:

- Mortgage
- Home equity line of credit
- Reverse mortgage
- Vehicle loans,
- Student loans, including those for others on which you co-signed.
- Personal loans
- Lawsuits or claims against you.
- Credit card balances
- Money borrowed informally from others.

Taxes are a liability, and we need to manage past filings and accompanying paperwork. This includes:

- Federal income taxes
- State income taxes
- Property taxes
- Other local taxes

You might find it helpful to organize this information by keeping different folders or sections for each account, and then referring to a master index list of accounts that are included in the primary letter of instructions so that it can be accessed and used by other people.

Wrapping Up The Book

We believe the most advantageous aspect of Fixed Indexed Annuity (FIA) plans their protection against losing money if the related index, such as the S&P 500 as example, declines. This ensures that the FIA's value remains the same even if the S&P 500 or some other linked indexes were to decline. This can be a simple drop of 1% – or it can even go up to 10% or 50%. In the end, the final product will remain the same.

The next beneficial function, in my opinion, is the Reset Feature of an FIA. I believe that it is rather powerful and helpful. At the completion of each contract period, the annuity's index value is subsequently and mechanically reset via the Reset Feature. The interest you've earned during the term will be "locked in," and you will not be able to lose it once the index value is reset.

In addition, you will not have any interest added to your account for the time in question if the relevant index, such as the S&P 500, finishes the term in negative territory. In other words, the value of your account does not decrease, and when the index value is reset, your account will begin tracking the index from that critical point. This will occur when the index value is restored. It is not essential that you allow the index to "get back to even" before you can start collecting interest on your investment.

There is a reset button on each and every FIA, though not all of these can be reset or revised at the end of the year. We opt for a system that features a yearly reset since we believe it offers the most potential for growth over the long term.

These are two characteristics that, for certain types of investors, could prove extremely desirable:

1. Downside protection of your money
2. Upside participation in the equity markets without the risk of loss.

The "REAL BENEFITS" of Index Annuities with the Annual Reset Design
A history of American Equity's Index-5* (9/30/98 - 9/30/16)

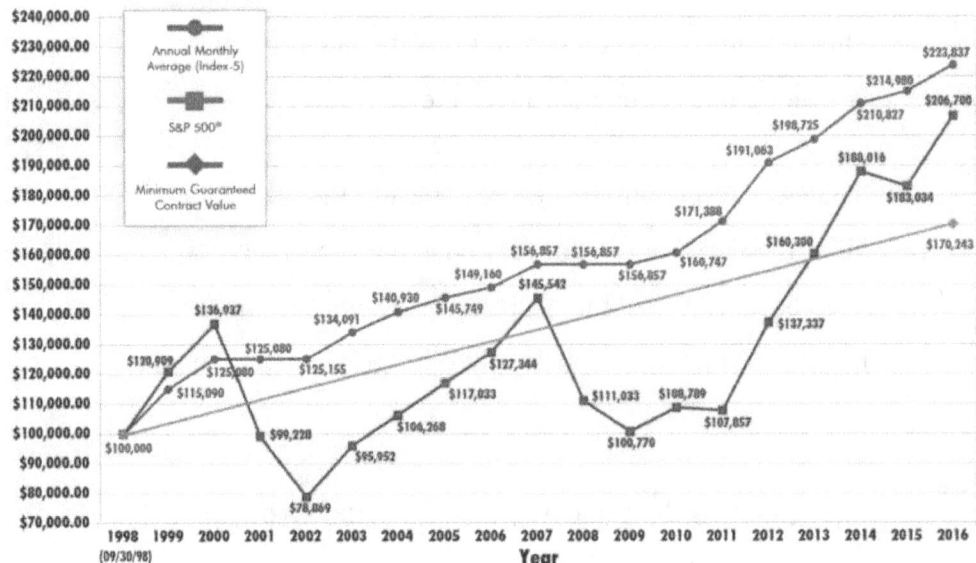

Source: American Equity Funds

For Example, only:

The growth of an investor's investment can be secured by modern FIAs, or a guaranteed income for life can be provided, or both growth and revenue can be provided. The following charts demonstrate how utilizing a fixed-indexed annuity can safeguard and grow your initial investment.

The following figures present a comparison between the annual returns of the S&P 500 over a period of 12 years and a fixed indexed annuity linked to the S&P 500 and has a **participation rate of 50% with no income cap**.

Year	S&P 500 Index Return	Fixed Indexed Annuity 50% Participation Rate, No Cap
2007	3.53%	1.77%
2008	-38.49%	0%
2009	23.45%	11.73%
2010	12.78%	6.39%
2011	-0.01%	0%
2012	13.41%	6.71%
2013	29.60%	14.80%
2014	11.39%	5.70%
2015	-0.73%	0%
2016	9.54%	4.77%
2017	19.42%	9.71%
2018	-6.24%	0%

And here is what the growth of a $500,000 investment looks like in the S&P 500 and in a Fixed Indexed Annuity looks like, based on the above criteria and returns.

Year	S&P 500 $500,000 Investment Return	Fixed Indexed Annuity Returns 50% Participation Rate, No Cap $500,000 Investment Return
2007	$517,650	$508,850
2008	$318,407	$508,850
2009	$393,073	$568,538
2010	$443,308	$604,868
2011	$443,263	$604,868
2012	$502,705	$645,454
2013	$651,506	$740,982
2014	$725,713	$783,217
2015	$720,415	$783,217
2016	$789,143	$820,577
2017	$942,394	$900,255
2018	$883,589	$900,255

FIAs vs. The Stock Market

Fixed Indexed Annuities aren't intended to provide returns that are higher than those of the market. They are constructed in such a way that they safeguard your initial investment while still enabling you to benefit from the upward trend of the stock market.

We try to avoid drawing parallels between them and the stock market since we are of the opinion that they were not intended to compete with the stock market. They are intended to compete with investments such as bonds, certificates of deposit, and others that have historically been less volatile. When you index your "safe" money (i.e., money that you are less comfortable putting at risk) to a growth tool like the S&P 500 while still maintaining principal protection, you have the potential for higher annual returns than other investments that are either less volatile or more secure, such as bonds or CDs. This is because indexing your "safe" money allows you to participate in the growth of the S&P 500.

The preceding illustration demonstrates how a financial instrument such as a fixed indexed annuity has the possibility to provide higher returns, especially in comparison to bonds or CDs, without taking on the volatility of, for instance, direct investment in the S&P 500. This is possible because the financial instrument is indexed to a specific index, such as the S&P 500.

Negative returns were experienced by the S&P 500 in the years 2008, 2011, 2015, and 2018. During that time, an FIA surely wouldn't have suffered any losses.

In the event that the S&P 500 index experiences a recovery, the value of your account will increase because you will be rewarded with a proportion of any favorable movement in the index. In the illustration that was just presented, the share of the total that you earn depends on a participation rate of 50%. There is no maximum, and the amount is reset every year. You do not take part in the market decreases, which is the primary benefit of the protection feature, but because of the "Reset Feature," you begin following the market from the point at which it was on the anniversary of your contract.

There is a possibility that some individuals, including customers and journalists covering finance, will take an anti-annuity stance. They might also get Fixed Indexed Annuities and Variable Annuities mixed up in their heads. Variable Annuities have been around for a significantly longer period of time than FIAs have, and in addition to being exposed to market risk, they also contain multiple levels of expenses.

On the other hand, the overwhelming majority of FIAs do not charge yearly fees, and none of the products offered by FIAs are subject to market risk.

The preceding illustration, in our opinion, makes a compelling case for the proposition that the appropriate fixed indexed retirement income can offer protection of principal, better returns in comparison to other fixed income products such as bonds, and the possibility of being considered as an essential component of a retirement plan.

FIAs in a Retirement Plan

Many retirees we speak to prefer understanding that a portion of their money is not subject to market risk but still has more potential for growth than cash or CDs. Given higher life expectancies, retirees may require a plan to build and safeguard their retirement savings. Sadly, many people are terrified of the stock market and losing large sums if they invest the money.

Some investment management organizations provide tactics that shift investors in and out of markets according to market volatility to avoid market crashes. Market timing. Timing the market to outperform or reduce the risk of inflation is unsuccessful and costly for most investors.

We recommend asset allocation for retirement savings. Asset allocation can match your goals, risk tolerance, and timeframe. **Our core planning and investment framework** helps clients do this.

Fixed Indexed Annuities are part of our Core Pillar. We emphasize on the uncapped, principal-protected, stock market upside, and yearly rest products.

The FIA may help you retire with confidence, security, and growth possibilities. While investors should avoid over-allocating assets to Fixed Indexed Annuities, many retirees may be satisfied to know that a part of their investment is secured with strong growth potential.

Fixed Index Annuities for Retirement

The FIA is a tool that can help bring you mental peace, security, and the possibility of growth throughout your retirement years. While we feel that investors should be cautious about over-allocating funds to Fixed Indexed Annuities, we also genuinely think that many retirees will be able to take comfort in the knowledge that a portion of their portfolio is secured with strong potential for development.

Why Do Retirees Buy Fixed Index Annuities?

A Fixed Index Annuity, abbreviated as FIA, is a contract that you and your life insurance provider enter into with one another. You make a payment known as a premium to the insurance company in exchange for receiving consistent income distributions over the course of a set amount of time, starting at some unspecified point in the future. Fixed index annuities are becoming increasingly important for newly retired individuals as a result of both rising life expectancies and falling pension levels.

Because people in the United States are living longer, it is critical to any retirement plan's effectiveness to ensure that one's savings are protected and that adequate income is guaranteed. The average American can anticipate living another 25 years or more when they reach retirement age. Sometimes people must live off of their retirement income for a longer period of time than they were actively employed and paid for throughout their working years. Pensions have historically been the primary source of financial security for retirees throughout their "golden years." Understanding the advantages of fixed index annuities is more crucial than it has ever been before due to the fact that the vast majority of firms no longer provide pensions for their employees.

You may benefit from purchasing a fixed index annuity by:

- Eliminate market losses.
- Having growth that is not taxable.
- Your savings should be protected, and you should earn retirement income that you can't outlast.
- Leave a legacy behind.
- Grow with deferred taxation!
- No contribution limits.
- If you transfer money prior to death, it will avoid being subject to probate.
- No loss in terms of the market's negative potential

A Closer Look at the Benefits

- **Stock market loss elimination** – An option to take part in the growth of the stock market is made available through fixed index annuities. When you buy a fixed-income investment account (FIA), your money can earn interest depending on fluctuations in an external index, such as the S&P 500 or the Nasdaq-100. This interest could be higher or lower than the index's value. You benefit from the option to share in any gains that the markets experience. Your contract value will not diminish even if the stock market experiences a decline.

- **Principal protection** – Your initial investment as well as any interest that has accrued, is 100% insured and covered by the insurance company against losses incurred from the stock market. You are guaranteed never to lose all the interest you have generated or the value of your premium.

- **Tax-deferred growth** – Contribution interest is tax-free till withdrawal. You are no longer required to pay federal income tax on annuity funds used for long-term care. Even if services aren't used, standard long-term-care insurance policies forfeit payments to insurance companies. Annuity holders can withdraw unspent monies. If you're too sick to qualify for long-term-care insurance, a long-term-care annuity may be easier to receive.

- **Income you can't outlive** – You can receive annuity income after a certain time. Several products increase income checks with inflation. Annuities can give emergency cash, death benefits, nursing home benefits, and lifetime income benefits, so the holder will never outlive the income from the annuity.

- **Provide a legacy with death benefits** – If you have a longer life expectancy, consider the financial impact on your family. Most people desire to leave a legacy. Fixed index annuities allow beneficiaries to inherit unspent funds tax-free.

How is a Fixed Index Annuity Different?

Unlike 401Ks and IRAs, annuities allow limitless contributions and tax-deferred growth. You can start taking revenue from your contract's accumulation value after 12 months or depending on your contract. The accumulation value is the total price paid plus 100% of interest generated less any withdrawals, submission charges, unpaid principal loans, and optional rider charges. Fixed index annuities provide bond-like income without interest rate risk. They also earn as the equities market increases without losing.

Including Fixed Index Annuities in Your Retirement Strategy

If you are searching for an investment plan for retirement that will safeguard your principle, has a significant upside, and will give a predictable, guaranteed lifelong income stream in retirement, an FIA is something that you may want to take into consideration as an option.

Retirement Industry Acronyms and Abbreviations

Here are some Acronyms, abbreviations, and definitions I would like to have at the end of the book for people to reference. Like many industries, the retirement profession is an acronym and abbreviation crazy. We have compiled this list of the more common acronyms, abbreviations, and definitions to help those unfamiliar with their meaning.

ABPT = Average Benefit Percentage Test

ABT = Average Benefits Test

ACA = Automatic Contribution Arrangement

ACP = Actual/Average Contribution Percentage

ADP = Actual/Average Deferral Percentage

ADR = Actual Deferral Ratio

AIF = Accredited Investment Fiduciary

AIFA = Accredited Investment Fiduciary Analyst

AGI = Adjusted Gross Income

ANPR = Advance Notice of Proposed Rulemaking

ARP = Association Retirement Plan

ATRA = American Taxpayer Relief Act of 2012

BD = Broker Dealers

BIC = Best Interest Contract

BICE = Best Interest Contract Exemption

BOPY = Beginning of Plan Year

CAA = Consolidated Appropriations Act of 2021

CEBS = Certified Employee Benefits Specialist

CFA = Chartered Financial Analyst

CFP = Certified Financial Planner

ChFC = Chartered Financial Consultant

CIA = Certified Internal Auditor

CIMA = Certified Investment Management Analyst

CIO = Chief Investment Officer

CIT = Collective Investment Trust

CLU = Chartered Life Underwriter

CMT = Chartered Market Technician

COBRA = Consolidated Omnibus Budget Reconciliation Act

CODA = Cash or Deferred Arrangement

COLA = Cost of Living Adjustment

CPA = Certified Public Accountant

CPC = Certified Pension Consultant

CRA = Certified Retirement Administrator

CRC = Certified Retirement Counselor

CRO = Chief Retirement Officer

CRSP = Certified Retirement Services Professional

CSP = Covered Service Provider

CTF = Common Trust Fund

CTPA = Compliance Third Party Administrators

CVA = Certified Valuation Analyst

CVRD = Coronavirus-Related Distributions

DB = Defined Benefit

DB(k) = Defined Benefit 401k combined plan

DC = Defined Contribution

DCIO = Defined Contribution Investment Only

DDQ = Due Diligence Questionnaires

DFVC = Delinquent Filer Voluntary Compliance program

DIA = Deferred Income Annuity

DIA = Designated Investment Alternative

DOL = Department of Labor

DOMA = Defense of Marriage Act

DPSP = Deferred Profit Sharing Plan

DRA = Deferred Retirement Annuities

DRO = Domestic Relations Order

EACA = Eligible Automatic Contribution Arrangement

EBAR = Equivalent Benefit Accrual Rate

EE = Employee

EESA = Emergency Economic Stabilization Act

EFT = Electronic Fund Transfer

EGTRRA = Economic Growth and Tax Relief Reconciliation Act of 2001

EIN = Employer Identification Number

EOPY = End of Plan Year

EPCRS = Employee Plans Compliance Resolution System

EPS = Education Policy Statement

ER = Employer

ERD = Eligible Rollover Distribution

ERISA = Employee Retirement Income Security Act

ERPA = Enrolled Retirement Plan Agent

ESG = Environmental, Social, Ethical and Governance

ESOP = Employee Stock Ownership Plan

ESPP = Employee Stock Purchase Plan

ETF = Exchange Traded Fund

ETI = Economically Targeted Investments

FAB = Field Assistance Bulletin, issued by the U.S. Department of Labor

FDL = Favorable Determination Letter

FIA = Fixed Indexed Annuity

FICA = Federal Insurance Contributions Act

FINRA = Financial Industry Regulatory Authority

FIT = Federal Income Tax

FLMI = Fellow of the Life Management Institute

FSA = Fellow of the Society of Actuaries

FT = Full-Time

GIC = Guaranteed Investment Contract

GIF = Guaranteed Investment Fund

GLIO = Guaranteed Lifetime Income Option

GLWB = Guaranteed Lifetime Withdrawal Benefit

GMWB = Guaranteed Minimum Withdrawal Benefits

GUST = An acronym that stands for a series of four tax laws that also made changes to how retirement plans operate.

HCE = Highly Compensated Employee

IA = Investment Analyst

IFC = Investment Fiduciary Consulting

IGVS = Investment Grade Value Stocks

IPS = Investment Policy Statement

IQPA = Independent Qualified Public Accountant

IRA = Individual Retirement Account

IRC = Internal Revenue Code

IRR = In-Plan Roth Rollover

IRS = Internal Revenue Service

IRT = In-Plan Roth Transfer

JEPPS = Joint Expert Panel on Pension Standards

KSOP = Combined ESOP and 401k Plan

LIMRA = Life Insurance Marketing and Research Association

LSD = Lump-Sum Distribution

LTPT = Long-Term Part-Time

LVP = Low Volatility Pension Plan

M&P = Master and Prototype

MCIM = Market Cycle Investment Management

MEP = Multiple Employer Plan

MMF = Money Market Fund

MPRA = Multiemployer Pension Reform Act

NAPA = National Association of Plan Advisors

NDCT = Nondiscriminatory Classification Test

NEC = Non-Elective Contribution

NHCE = Non-Highly Compensated Employee

NQDC = Non-Qualified Deferred Compensation

NRA = Normal Retirement Age

NUA = Net Unrealized Appreciation

OAR = Outsourced Administrative Responsibilities

OIAI = Once-in-always-in

OPEB = Other Post Employment Benefits

ORP = Optional Retirement Plan

PBGC = Pension Benefit Guaranty Corporation

PDT = Permissive Disaggregation Test

PEO = Professional Employer Organization

PEP = Pooled Employer Plan

PII = Personally Identifiable Information

PIN = Personal Identification Number

PLR = Private Letter Ruling

PPA = Pension Protection Act of 2006

PPACA = Patient Protection and Affordable Care Act

PPP = Pooled Plan Provider

PT = Part-Time

PTE = Prohibited Transaction Exemption

PY = Plan Year

PYE = Plan Year-End

QAB = Quality Assurance Bulletin issued by the IRS

QACA = Qualified Automatic Contribution Arrangement

QBAD = Qualified Birth and Adoption Distribution

QDIA = Qualified Default Investment Alternative

QDRO = Qualified Domestic Relations Order

QJSA = Qualified Joint And Survivor Annuity

QKA = Qualified 401k Administrator

QLAC = Qualified Lifetime Annuity Contract or Qualifying Longevity Annuity Contract

QMAC = Qualified Matching Contribution

QNEC = Qualified Non-Elective Contribution

QOSA = Qualified Optional Survivor Annuity

QPA = Qualified Pension Administrator

QPAM = Qualified Professional Asset Manager

QPDA = Qualified Plan Distributed Annuity

QPFC = Qualified Plan Financial Consultant

QPLO = Qualified Plan Loan Offset

QPSA = Qualified Pre=retirement Survivor Annuity

QSAT = Questionnaire Self-Audit Tool

QSLOB = Qualified Separate Lines of Business

QTA = Qualified Termination Administrator

QTIP = Qualified Terminable Interest Property

RAP = Remedial Amendment Procedure

RBD = Required Beginning Date

REIT = Real Estate Investment Trust

RFI = Request for Information

RFP = Request for Proposal

RIA = Registered Investment Advisor

RIG = Retirement Income Generator

RMD = Required Minimum Distribution

RPA = Retirement Plans Associate

RPF = Responsible Plan Fiduciaries

RRIF = Registered Retirement Income Fund (Canada)

SAR = Summary Annual Report

SARSEP = Salary Reduction Simplified Employee Pension Plan

SBJCA = Small Business Jobs and Credit Act of 2010

SBJPA = Small Business Job Protection Act

SCOTUS = Supreme Court of the United States

SCP = Self-Correction Program

SDBA = Self-Directed Brokerage Account

SECURE = Setting Every Community Up for Retirement
Enhancement Act of 2019

SEP = Simplified Employee Pension

SEPP = Substantially Equal Periodic Payment

SHMAC = Safe Harbor Match Contribution

SHNEC = Safe Harbor Non-Elective Contribution

SIMPLE = Savings Incentive Match Plan for Employees (of Small Employers)

SMM = Summary of Material Modifications

SPD = Summary Plan Description

SSA = Social Security Administration

SSN = Social Security Number

SSP = State-Based Savings Programs

TAA = Tactical Asset Allocation

TAMRA = Technical and Miscellaneous Revenue Act

TCJA = Tax Cuts and Jobs Act

TDF = Target-Date Fund

TEFRA = Technical and Miscellaneous Revenue Act

TFSA = Tax-Free Savings Account (Canada)

TPA = Third Party Administrator

TRA = Taxpayer Relief Act of 1997

TRO = Total Retirement Outsourcing

TSA = Tax-sheltered Annuity

UPIA = Uniform Prudent Investment Act

USERRA = Uniformed Services Employment and Reemployment Rights Act

VFCP = Voluntary Fiduciary Compliance Program

VIA = Variable Immediate Annuity

VRU = Voice Response Unit

VS = Volume Submitter

WFTRA = Working Families Tax Relief Act of 2004

WRERA = The Worker, Retiree and Employer Recovery Act of 2008

YOS = Year of Service

Glossary: Your Guide to Retirement Terminology

Saving for retirement should be simple. But whether you're an employer sponsoring a 401(k) plan or an employee just trying to save, it can feel like the price of entry is an economics degree.

Put some of the blame on retirement's complex terminology. Just look at the language used by the experts: fiduciaries, vesting cliffs, summary plan descriptions, distributions — it's enough to make you want to pour yourself a tall glass of liquidity and rollover.

Guideline believes that saving for retirement should be easy for everyone. Let's help you clear a few things up. Consider this glossary your secret decoder ring to all things retirement – 401(k) and beyond.

401(k) Plan

A popular, employer-sponsored retirement plan is offered as an employee benefit. Traditionally, money is taken directly from employees' paychecks pre-tax, deposited in the plan's trust, growing tax-deferred, and is not taxed until withdrawal.

Alternatively, the employee may elect to have the amount taken after tax, deposited in the trust, and invested and withdrawn on a tax-free basis.

Annual Rate of Return

Your annual rate of return is the percent change in your account due to investment gains or losses over the course of a year. Expressed as a percentage, this number can vary widely based on your investment choices and strategy—though according to some, the average annual return is 5% to 8%.

Assets Under Management (AUM) Fee

These are fees that investment advisers and mutual funds charge as a percentage of the money they're managing on your behalf. These might look like a tiny percentage (1.63% is the industry average[1]), but their cumulative effect can cost retirement account holders thousands of dollars over the long run.

Auto-IRA

Even if an employee doesn't have access to a 401(k) plan, their employer may be able to enroll them into a state-run retirement account called an "auto-IRA." This is actually a requirement in some states (e.g., Illinois Secure Choice). Scroll below to learn how individual retirement accounts (IRAs) work.

Automatic Enrollment

While some companies leave it up to employees to sign up for their retirement plan (opt-in), others automatically enroll them by default. Though employees have the option to back out any time, they tend not to. Companies with automatic enrollment (sometimes called "auto-enrollment") average a very high 92% plan participation rate.

Automatic Rebalancing

You've heard the saying, "buy low, sell high." While you can micromanage your retirement savings, doing so isn't practical. Automatic rebalancing is a retirement feature that rebalances your account automatically. This involves adjusting your portfolio's percentage of stocks, bonds, cash, and other investments back to your original stated target.

Compound Interest

Think of compound interest as the "interest on the interest" that your investments earn. If you invest $100 and earn 10% interest in your first year, you'll have $110 to invest in the second year, $121 in the third, and so on. In this example, if you continue earning 10% interest every year, you will double your money in seven years. [2] Sometimes called "compounding," this effect makes it possible for even a modest retirement account to grow significantly over a career.

Cal Savers

A California retirement program requires employers with five or more California-based employees to offer a retirement plan.

Cliff Vesting

While some companies allow 401(k) plan participants to vest in their full employer contributions account gradually, others prefer a more abrupt formula. In cliff vesting, employees remain 0% vested in their employer contributions account until they complete a minimum number of years of service when they become 100% vested. A typical cliff vesting schedule uses three years of service.

Deferrals

Also called employee contributions, deferrals are the portion of an employee's paycheck set aside for their retirement account. Deferrals might be expressed as either a set dollar amount or a percentage. In some cases, a company might automatically assign an employee a default deferral rate (see automatic enrollment). Even then, employees can update their deferrals at any time.

Defined Benefit Plan

Commonly referred to as a pension, this is an arrangement where retired employees are paid a guaranteed monthly income from their employers, who choose the plan's investments.

Defined Contribution Plan

This is a retirement plan in which employer contributions are defined and allocated to the individual accounts of each employee. 401(k) plans are a type of defined contribution plan where participants can contribute a percentage or set amount from their paychecks every pay period. Employer contributions in a 401(k) plan are optional.

Distribution

When you withdraw money from your retirement account for any reason, that's called a distribution. While this technically includes situations where you might be moving funds from one plan to another (see "rollover"), in most contexts, distributions are taken for the immediate benefit of the account holder. In most cases, you'll owe federal and state income taxes on the amount. In addition, if you take a distribution before turning 59 ½ (yes, the law's that specific), you'll owe the Feds an additional 10% early distribution penalty. Some states may also impose an early distribution penalty (e.g., California's is 2.5%). [3]

Dollar-Cost Averaging

Dollar-cost averaging is a strategy that involves investing the same amount of money on a periodic schedule (e.g., monthly). While the number of shares bought may fluctuate from month to month, the amount invested does not. During periods of price declines, you're automatically buying more shares than when prices are higher. If you set aside money for retirement every paycheck, you're naturally benefiting from dollar-cost averaging.

Employee Contribution Limits

The IRS caps how much individuals can set aside in their retirement accounts per year. These contribution limits vary depending on the kind of account. As of 2022, the 401(k)-contribution limit for individuals is $20,500. If you turn 50 (or older) in 2022, you're eligible to contribute an additional $6,500.[4] IRA account holders are limited to much smaller contribution limits. In either case, it's important to note that employer contributions do not count towards this cap.

Employer-Sponsored Retirement Plan

While individuals can open retirement accounts on their own (see our explanation of IRAs), employers can also offer their employees access to a plan, usually with the help of a third-party provider. A 401(k) plan is one of the most popular employer-sponsored retirement plans.

Employer Matching

If a 401(k) plan has an "employer match," that means the employer will contribute to an employee's retirement account based on how much that employee defers. Simply, the more the employee contributes, the more the employer does, up to a maximum cap determined by the employer. Employer contributions are tax-deductible for employers up to applicable deduction limits, making them a popular way for companies to reward their employees.

Employee Retirement Income Security Act (ERISA)

Call it the closest thing to a 401(k) rulebook. While the federal government doesn't require companies to offer retirement plans, it does set minimum standards for those that do. The Employee Retirement Income Security Act (ERISA) outlines the conduct, responsibilities, and obligations 401(k) providers have to their employees. It also requires most retirement plans to pass stringent nondiscrimination testing to ensure that top executives aren't disproportionately benefiting compared to other employees.

Expense Ratio

Most 401(k) plans offer participants control over the investment of their accounts by selecting from among a menu of mutual funds. Each mutual fund in a participant's portfolio comes with an administrative and operating charge, taken from the participant's invested funds as a percentage of the assets invested in that fund. This charge is called the fund's "expense ratio." A fund's expense ratio measures how much of a fund's assets are taken by the fund's manager for these purposes, and it can vary widely from fund to fund. Some funds charge an expense ratio loaded with high fees. For example, if your account has $30,000 and that entire amount is invested in a fund with a 1% expense ratio, your account is paying $300 in fees each year for that fund. If you want to evaluate a plan by how costly it is, consider comparing the expense ratio, as disclosed in the fund's prospectus, for each fund in the plan's menu.

Fiduciary

Fiduciaries are individuals or entities entrusted with handling funds or other assets belonging to someone else or exercising discretion in administrative activities. When it comes to retirement plans, there are a few different kinds of fiduciaries — but generally speaking, they're the ones managing your company's 401(k) plan, making benefit determinations, interpreting the plan document, and/or selecting the plan's fund menu, or providing investment advice to those who make those decisions. Fiduciaries are legally obligated to make decisions solely in the interest of plan participants and their beneficiaries.

Form 5500

Each year, 401(k) plan sponsors are required to file Form 5500 with the federal government. This annual report outlines basic information about the sponsor's business, its retirement plans, total participants, and other details. The document is typically accompanied by secondary forms or "schedules" with additional detail. Sponsors with at least 100 employees are required to attach an audited financial statement as well, while sponsors with fewer than 100 employees may be able to fill out a shorter version of the form.

Graded Vesting

Employers may gradually allow 401(k) plan participants to vest in the employer's contributions over time (e.g., 20% after one year, 40% after two years). This approach is called graded vesting. Federal law mandates that it can't take longer than six years for employees to vest 100% of their match.

Hardship Withdrawal

Your retirement account wasn't designed to serve as a personal rainy-day fund. That said, some retirement plans allow for participants to take "hardship withdrawals" for certain circumstances, like to pay for medical expenses or to purchase a primary residence (sorry, no summer homes). In most cases, hardship withdrawals are subject to federal and state income taxes. Plus, if you're not yet age 59½, there is a federal early distribution tax penalty of 10%. Some states may also impose an early distribution penalty (e.g., California's is 2.5%).

Highly Compensated Employee (HCE)

For the 2022 plan year, an employee earned over $135,000 in 2021 and (if the plan administrator chooses to use this criterion) ranks among a company's top 20% in compensation, is considered a highly compensated employee (HCE) by the IRS. If they own more than a 5% stake in the business or are an employee with a family relationship to someone that does, in either 2021 or 2022, they're also considered an HCE for 2022 regardless of pay. The distinction between HCEs and the rest of a company's population matters in the context of nondiscrimination testing.

Individual Retirement Plan (IRA)

While 401(k) plans are offered by employers, individual retirement accounts (IRAs) are — you guessed it — only available to individuals. IRAs offer many of the same tax benefits as conventional employer-sponsored plans, though participants are only allowed to contribute a much smaller amount ($6,000 per year for individuals as of 2022, plus an additional $1,000 if age 50 or over in 2022).

Illinois Secure Choice

An Illinois retirement program requires employers in Illinois who have been in business for two or more years to enroll their employees into a state-managed IRA.

Liquidity

In short, liquidity refers to the immediate usability of an asset. If you've got cash in your wallet, that's "liquid" — you could easily spend that money if you wanted to. Retirement accounts aren't considered liquid until you reach retirement age because you can't take distributions while employed, unless your plan allows for hardship withdrawals or other such special circumstances without a penalty, absent loans, hardship withdrawals, etc.

Loan

Individuals can sometimes borrow money from their 401(k) account and gradually pay it back. Rules and eligibility requirements vary from plan to plan, but unlike hardship withdrawals, IRS taxes and penalties don't apply to 401(k) loans unless you default on them.

Mutual Fund

"Mutual fund" might sound like Wall Street jargon, but it's a simple concept. A mutual fund is a pool of investors' money that's subsequently invested in stocks, bonds, and other securities and is managed by someone else (a fund manager). A mutual fund is structured to achieve certain investment objectives as defined in its prospectus. Mutual funds don't put investors' eggs in one basket — meaning if one specific stock goes under, the damage is limited. This quality makes them a popular investment option for retirement accounts.

Nondiscrimination Testing

By law, a company's 401(k) plan can't favor owners, executives, or those making the most money. Annual nondiscrimination tests look at employee participation, employer contributions, and other factors to determine if the plan is compliant with those requirements.

Certain retirement plans (see Safe Harbor) automatically satisfy some nondiscrimination testing rules.

Oregon Saves

An Oregon retirement program that requires all employers to facilitate the state auto-IRA program if they don't offer a retirement plan for their Oregon-based employees.

Pre-Tax Contributions

Depending on the plan, employees can either contribute to their retirement account before or after federal and state taxes are taken out of their paycheck. As the name suggests, pre-tax 401(k) contributions are taken out before. Thus, they reduce the employee's gross income in that year, potentially lowering income taxes. See "Traditional 401(k) plan" for greater detail.

Profit-Sharing

In the context of retirement, profit sharing involves an employer making tax-deductible contributions that are allocated to employees' 401(k) accounts. Think of it as a bonus deposited directly into employees' retirement accounts. Profit-sharing comes with a slew of benefits for employers and employees.

Portability

Portability refers to the ease with which you can transfer an employee's account from one employer's plan to the plan of a different employer after a job change. In other words, if you contribute to a 401(k) account at your current job, you'll have the option of rolling over that account to an IRA or future employer's retirement plan (assuming the future employer's plan permits such rollovers).

Portfolio

This term simply represents your overall collection of investments. A diverse retirement portfolio features stocks, bonds, commodities, mutual funds, and other investments. The mix of these reflects how aggressive or conservative an investment strategy is.

Qualified Distributions

Individuals can only take money out of their retirement account when specific events (such as death, disability, termination of employment or at retirement age, or, if the plan permits, financial hardship) occur. These are called qualified distributions. Except in the case of Roth 401(k) plans and Roth IRAs, those distributions are subject to tax and sometimes the early distribution penalty discussed above.[3]

Required Minimum Distribution (RMD)

While being "hands-off" on your retirement savings is usually a good thing, eventually, you do need to dip into those funds. In the case of HCEs, the IRS requires individuals in their early 70s to begin drawing down their 401(k) accounts and pay taxes on these amounts, whether or not they terminate their employment. Employees who are not HCEs but have attained the RMD age may defer taxation until after they terminate their employment. These are called required minimum distributions (RMDs).

Rollover

When you move your retirement savings from one plan to another
(as might be the case when switching employers), that's called a
rollover. If the old and new employers share the same third-party
401(k) plan provider, the transfer is a simple one. In all other cases,
the old provider will likely directly transfer the value of the account
in cash to the new plan.

Roth 401(k) Plan

Roth 401(k) plans allow employees to contribute to their retirement
accounts on an "after-tax" basis, meaning they won't owe taxes on
that money or the investment income on that money when they
retire. Roth accounts tend to be a popular option for younger
employees since they have more time for their earnings to
compound (see compound interest).

Roth IRA

Roth IRAs allow individuals to contribute to their retirement
accounts on an "after-tax" basis, meaning they won't owe taxes on
qualified distributions (including any earnings) that are withdrawn
from the IRA when they retire. Unlike 401(k) plans, IRAs are not
necessarily employer-sponsored.

Safe Harbor 401(k) Plans

Companies that offer retirement plans are subject to many
compliance requirements, including nondiscrimination testing. Safe
Harbor plans are a special kind of 401(k) plan that automatically
satisfies some nondiscrimination tests. As a trade-off, these plans

require companies to contribute a minimum amount to their employees' retirement accounts.

Simplified Employee Pension (SEP)

SEP stands for Simplified Employee Pension Plan, which is a type of individual retirement account (IRA) where contributions are made by the employer only. SEPs are tax-deferred retirement plans that may be established by businesses of any size. They are generally popular with entrepreneurs and small business owners due to larger contribution limits, greater flexibility, and fewer administration requirements compared to other retirement plans. If you own a company without many employees and want a low-stress, flexible way to contribute to retirement, a SEP IRA may be a good fit. Learn more about SEP IRAs here, as well as how SEP differs from a 401(k).

Summary Plan Description (SPD)

By law, companies with retirement plans are required to provide employees with an overview of the program that is written in language designed to be understood by the average participant. How the plan works, eligibility requirements, vesting details, and other important details need to be included.

Target-Date Fund

Mutual funds designed to invest funds in a manner to help achieve the investor's investment objectives at a specific point in time are called target-date funds. In the context of retirement, a target date fund's strategy typically gets more conservative the closer an individual gets to retirement age.

Tax-Deferred

If you own a 401(k) account, your investment earnings are growing on a "tax-deferred" basis. This means that, unlike in a normal taxable investment account, you won't pay taxes on earnings in your account every year. When it comes time to retire, you'll just owe income taxes on what you take out.

Tax Penalty

If you take out retirement funds before turning 59½ years old, you'll do so at a cost. The IRS will assess a 10% fee (a tax penalty) in addition to federal and state income taxes. Some states may impose a similar tax (e.g., California's is 2.5%).

Traditional 401(k) Plan

Traditional 401(k) retirement plans allow participants to set aside a share of their paycheck on a pre-tax basis. This means that the IRS can only tax these funds when the individual receives a distribution from the plan, with the possible exception of the RMD discussed above, where taxation is imposed on an HCE even if the required minimum amount is not distributed.

Traditional IRA

Traditional IRAs are tax-advantaged accounts at a bank, insurance company, or other regulated financial institution that allow individuals to contribute money on a pre-tax basis. This means that the IRS can only tax these funds when the individual receives a distribution from the account. Unlike 401(k) plans, IRAs are not necessarily employer-sponsored.

Voluntary Open Multiple Employer Plan
Small businesses, under the coordination of a third party, can be bundled together under one retirement plan. This arrangement gives them more competitive pricing but provides less room for plan customization.

Voluntary Payroll Deduction IRA
As an alternative to a 401(k) plan, companies can help their employees enroll in a voluntary payroll deduction IRA. Individuals establish an IRA, and the employer's only responsibility is to facilitate the transfer of the employees' contributions from their paychecks to their IRA accounts.

Workplace Retirement Plan
Companies often offer their employees access to a retirement account as a benefit. A traditional 401(k) plan is the most popular example of a workplace retirement plan.

www.ingramcontent.com/pod-product-compliance
Lightning Source LLC
Chambersburg PA
CBHW070349220526
45467CB00001B/308